Steck-Vaughn

Vocabulary
Connections

Harcourt Achieve
Rigby · Saxon · Steck-Vaughn

www.HarcourtAchieve.com
1.800.531.5015

ILLUSTRATIONS

Cover: Ed Lindlof
Content Area Logos: Skip Sorvino

Donna Ayers 60–63, 65; Doron Ben-Ami 67–68, 70; Heidi Chang 26, 28, 52, 120–122, 124; Nancy Carpenter 79–81, 96–98, 100; Eldon Doty 36–39, 41, 46, 72–74, 76, 85–87, 89, 103–105, 107; Leslie Dunlap 18–20, 31–33, 35; Doris Ettlinger 12–15, 17; Bob Lange 24–25, 48, 50, 90–92, 94; Jim McConnell 7–9, 11, 108–111, 113; Den Schofield 115–116, 118; Jean & Mou-sien Tseng 56–57, 59.

PHOTOGRAPHY

P. 6 © Leonard Lee Rue, III/Photo Researchers, Inc.; p. 23 © Johns Hopkins Children's Center; p. 29 © McLaughlin/The Image Works; p. 42a © Courtesy, National Center for Missing and Exploited Children; p. 42b © Kevin Kornemann/Getty Images; p. 43 © Leonard Freed/Magnum Photos, Inc.; p. 44 © Nancy Burson; pp. 47, 49 © Naval Photographic Center; p. 53 © Chuck O'Rear/Westlight; pp. 54–55 © Rene Burri/Magnum Photos, Inc.; p. 66 © NPS photo by Peter Jones; p. 71 © Micheal Nichols/Magnum Photos, Inc.; p.77 © Spectrum Colour Library/Westlight; p. 78 © Lawrence Migdale/ Photo Researchers, Inc.; p. 83 © Ellis Herwig/Stock, Boston; p. 84 © s Newsphotos; p. 95 © George Holton/Photo Researchers, Inc.; p. 101 © Philip Wallick/The Stock Market; p. 102 © Peter Arnold; p. 114, 130b © AP Photo/Mississippi State Univ./Fred Faulk; p. 119 © Carson Baldwin, Jr./FPG International.

Additional photography by PhotoDisc/Getty Royalty Free.

ACKNOWLEDGMENTS

Robert F. Burgess: Excerpt from "Lindbergh and the Underground Lake" condensed from *The Cave Divers* by Robert F. Burgess. Copyright © 1976. Originally published by Dodd, Mead & Company. Reprinted by permission of the author.

Macmillan Publishing Company: Pronunciation Key, reprinted with permission of the publisher from the *Macmillan School Dictionary 2.* Copyright © 1990 Macmillan Publishing Company, a division of Macmillan, Inc.

Copyright © 1980 by Joan Davenport Carris. From the book THE REVOLT OF 10-X published by Harcourt Brace Jovanovich, Inc. Reprinted by permission of McIntosh and Otis, Inc.

From AN AUTOBIOGRAPHY by Agatha Christie, copyright © 1977 by Agatha Christie Limited. Used by permission of G. P. Putnam's Sons, a division of Penguin Group (USA) Inc. Reprinted by permission of Harold Ober Associates Incorporated.

From THE DISCOVERERS by Daniel J. Boorstin, copyright © 1983 by Daniel J. Boorstin. Used by permission of Random House, Inc.

Russell & Volkening, Inc.: From "Alfred Nobel: Dynamite and Prizes" from *Trail Blazers of Technology* by Harland Manchester. Copyright © 1962 by Harland Manchester. Reprinted by the permission of Russell & Volkening as agents for the author.

TABLE OF CONTENTS

GREAT CONNECTIONS

Connections, like this land bridge, are everywhere. A tunnel, microscope, and brain surgeon are connections, too. All of them open up new worlds for humanity.

In Lessons 1–4, you will read about some great connections that have linked two things together in a new way. Think about how a tunnel bridges the distance between two places. What other things or discoveries serve as connections? Which people, places, or concepts have they brought closer? Write your ideas under the headings below.

Connections	What They Connect

★ Read the story below. Think about the meanings of the **boldfaced** words. ★

A Bridge to America

When Columbus discovered America in 1492, he had to make the journey by ship across a vast ocean. But many scientists believe that the first people who inhabited North America were able to walk here. How was this possible? After all, one look at the map will tell you that no other continent is **adjacent** to the Americas. The nearest land is the eastern end of Russia, and it is separated from Alaska by thirty-six miles of icy, arctic water.

However, we now know that this narrow **strait** in the Bering Sea was not always there. Fourteen thousand years ago, when the world was locked in an ice age, ice covered many of the northern **latitudes** of the globe. Because so much of the earth's water was frozen, the oceans shrank. So the land beneath what is now the Bering Sea was exposed. It formed a "land bridge" that linked the two continents and permitted the **forebears**, or ancestors, of today's Native Americans to walk to America.

While no one can prove that wandering, **nomadic**, tribes once traveled this path, scientists have **demonstrated** that the land bridge did exist. They know that the region was not always under water because they have found fossils of land plants and animal bones in the Bering Sea. At one time, the Bering Sea was a vast grass-covered plain, inhabited by bison, horses, and giant mammoths.

The evidence for the land bridge makes it a **probable** route to North America. In addition, there is other stronger evidence for the theory that the first Americans came from Asia. Racially, Asians are closely related to modern Native Americans. In addition, many Native American implements, customs, and legends resemble those of prehistoric Asians. Therefore, it seems likely that modern Native Americans are the **descendants** of prehistoric Asians.

One question still remains. Why did they come here? Since these early Asians were **migrants**, it seems possible that they might have accidentally wandered into America in search of better hunting grounds. Whatever their reasons, they brought a new people and culture to a largely empty, **uninhabited** continent. Without this bridge to America, our country might be a very different place today.

★ Go back to the story. Underline the words or sentences that give you a clue to the meaning of each **boldfaced** word. ★

CONTEXT CLUES

In each sentence a word or phrase is underlined. Choose a word from the box to replace that word or phrase. Write the word on the line.

strait	probable	forebears	demonstrated
adjacent	latitudes	migrants	uninhabited
nomadic	descendants		

1. According to many scientists, it is <u>reasonable to believe</u> that people from Asia crossed a land bridge and entered North America at least 12,000 years ago. _____

2. They came from northeast Asia, the land <u>lying next</u> to what is modern-day Alaska. _____

3. These tribes were <u>constantly wandering</u> people who eventually moved south through areas of Canada into what is now the United States. _____

4. As they entered warmer <u>regions to the north or south of the equator</u>, there were major differences in the climate and natural surroundings. _____

5. These <u>roving people</u> saw plains and huge forests of spruce and fir. _____

6. These lands had been <u>not lived in</u> by people and were overflowing with animals, fish, and many different kinds of plants.

_____

7. The <u>ancestors</u> of today's Native Americans became skillful hunters and fishers. _____

8. Like their <u>offspring who would come after them</u>, they respected the land around them and the animals living on it, and they took only what they needed to survive. _____

9. As they <u>proved by their actions</u>, they were prepared to meet the challenges of this new environment. _____

10. The wandering spirit of these Asian peoples had taken them far away from the <u>narrow channel connecting two larger bodies of water</u> that they first crossed to enter this new world.

_____

ANALOGIES

An **analogy** compares two pairs of words. The relationship between the first pair of words is the same as the relationship between the second pair of words. For example: <u>Finger</u> is to <u>hand</u> as <u>toe</u> is to <u>foot</u>. Use the words in the box to complete the following analogies.

probable	**uninhabited**	**adjacent**
strait	**forebears**	

1. <u>Near</u> is to <u>far</u> as _____ is to <u>distant</u>.

2. <u>Pass</u> is to <u>mountains</u> as _____ is to <u>seas</u>.

3. <u>Clan</u> is to <u>family</u> as _____ are to <u>forefathers</u>.

4. <u>Complete</u> is to <u>finish</u> as _____ is to <u>likely</u>.

5. <u>Barren</u> is to <u>lush</u> as _____ is to <u>populated</u>.

WORD PAIRS

Words with similar parts may have related meanings. Study each word pair. Think about how the meanings of the words are alike. Check the meanings in the Dictionary. Then write a sentence for each word.

1. **migrant — migration**

_____

_____

2. **demonstrate — demonstrative**

_____

_____

3. **nomad — nomadic**

_____

_____

4. **uninhabited — uninhabitable**

_____

_____

5. **descend — descendant**

_____

_____

WORD GAME

The underlined letters in each sentence below can be used in one of the vocabulary words. Use the underlined letters and the context of the sentence to determine the correct vocabulary word. Write the word on the line.

nomadic	uninhabited	forebears	probable
latitudes	strait	descendants	adjacent
demonstrated	migrants		

1. The ad says there is a house right next to our store that is for sale.

   _____

2. I know that it is possible to travel from the Atlantic Ocean to the Pacific Ocean, but I cannot seem to find water linking the two seas on this map.

   _____

3. When you are at the equator, you know there are regions to the north and to the south that will have similar climates.

   _____

4. My grandparents used to hunt bears in the woods near our farm, but the animals have long since been frightened away by too many people.

   _____

5. I have a friend who gets mad whenever anyone suggests to him that he should settle down and stop wandering from job to job.

   _____

6. The singer cut a demo to show his singing style and to try to prove to the record company that he had talent. _____

7. It's unlikely that anyone can rob the house because locks were installed on all the doors and windows. _____

8. Many animals have ancestors that looked quite different from them, but it's hard to believe that ants ever looked any different than they do today. _____

9. It has become a habit with us to look for quiet beaches where we will not see other people. _____

10. The dogs ran from house to house, looking for a family that would take them in. _____

Directions: Read each sentence. Pick the word that best completes the sentence. Mark the answer space for that word.

Be sure to mark the answer space correctly. Do <u>not</u> mark the circle with an X or with a checkmark (✓). Instead, fill in the circle neatly and completely with your pencil.

GW_VC04_PE_H_p10

1. The _____ of today's Native Americans were adventurers.
   Ⓐ traveling   Ⓒ nomadic
   Ⓑ forebears   Ⓓ hunters

2. The musicians _____ their talent with a wonderful performance.
   Ⓕ showing   Ⓗ adjacent
   Ⓖ sang   Ⓙ demonstrated

3. Farm workers who travel from place to place looking for work are called _____.
   Ⓐ latitudes   Ⓒ move
   Ⓑ picking   Ⓓ migrants

4. As far as scientists know, nearby planets are _____ by people.
   Ⓕ uninhabited   Ⓗ descendants
   Ⓖ probable   Ⓙ auctioned

5. The family crossed the _____ in a large sailboat.
   Ⓐ desert   Ⓒ mountainous
   Ⓑ uninhabited   Ⓓ strait

6. There are _____ cultures around the world whose wandering ways make their lives very different from ours.
   Ⓕ descendants   Ⓗ nomadic
   Ⓖ move   Ⓙ forebears

7. Countries that are located in the _____ near the equator have a warm climate.
   Ⓐ migrants   Ⓒ swam
   Ⓑ latitudes   Ⓓ poles

8. It is very _____ that the dog came looking for a biscuit.
   Ⓕ probable   Ⓗ hungry
   Ⓖ uninhabited   Ⓙ sadly

9. The Wongs bought the house _____ to ours.
   Ⓐ probable   Ⓒ strait
   Ⓑ adjacent   Ⓓ distance

10. Their _____ still live in the same part of the world.
    Ⓕ descendants   Ⓗ demonstrated
    Ⓖ wandering   Ⓙ relationships

Review

1. The pioneers in the American West _____ many dangers and hardships.
   Ⓐ confronted   Ⓒ fearlessness
   Ⓑ wrath   Ⓓ greeting

2. _____ was a likely characteristic of these people.
   Ⓕ Pumice   Ⓗ Inhale
   Ⓖ Confronted   Ⓙ Fearlessness

3. These people depended on _____ with one another to survive.
   Ⓐ accumulate   Ⓒ cooperation
   Ⓑ colleagues   Ⓓ fight

4. A _____ influence in their lives was the weather.
   Ⓕ dominant   Ⓗ nothing
   Ⓖ adviser   Ⓙ weakness

Think about what it must have been like for the early Asians when they arrived in North America, a totally uninhabited land. They had to create everything they needed to survive with their own hands.

Imagine what it would be like to live in an uninhabited place, such as a remote island. Think about the things you use every day that would be unavailable in such a place. In a paragraph, describe what you think your life would be like on an uninhabited island. Explain how you would go about getting the food, clothing, and shelter needed to survive. Use some vocabulary words in your writing.

_____

_____

_____

_____

_____

_____

Turn to "My Personal Word List" on page 131. Write some words from the story or other words that you would like to know more about. Use a dictionary to find the meanings.

_____

_____

_____

_____

★ Read the story below. Think about the meanings of
the **boldfaced** words. ★

New Worlds Within

Antoni van Leeuwenhoek believed that powerful microscopes could
change the world. He proved it by discovering the world within.

The same suspicions that made Galileo's critics unwilling to look
through his telescope, and then reluctant to believe what they saw, also
cursed the microscope. The telescope was obviously useful in battle,
but there were no battles yet where the microscope could help. In the
absence of a science of optics, sensible people were especially wary of
"optical illusions." This medieval distrust of all optical devices was the
great obstacle to a science of optics. And to a certain extent the crude
microscopes in those days confirmed their suspicions.

Just as the telescope had brought together the earth and the most
distant heavenly bodies into a single scheme of thought, now
microscopic **vistas** revealed a **minuscule** world surprisingly like that
seen on a large scale every day.

The microscope opened dark continents never before entered and in
many ways easy to explore. The great sea voyages had required large
capital, organizing genius, talents of leadership, and the **charisma** of a
Prince Henry or a Columbus, a Magellan or a Gama. **Astronomic**
exploring required the **coordinated** observations of people in many
places. But a lone man anywhere with a microscope could venture for
the first time where there were neither experienced navigators nor
skilled pilots.

Antoni van Leeuwenhoek (1632–1723) with his microscope
pioneered this new science of other-worldly exploration. In Delft, where
he was born, his father made baskets to pack the famous delftware for
the world market. Antoni himself made a good living by selling silk,
wool, cotton, buttons, and ribbons to the city's comfortable burghers,
and had a substantial income as head of the City Council, inspector of
weights and measures, and court surveyor. He was a close friend of Jan
Vermeer, and on the painter's death was appointed **trustee** of Vermeer's
bankrupt estate. He never attended a university, and during his whole
ninety years he left the Netherlands only twice, journeying once to
Antwerp and once to England.

Careful drapers like Leeuwenhoek were in the habit of using a
low-power magnifying glass to inspect the quality of cloth. His first

microscope was a small lens, ground by hand from a glass globule and clamped between two **perforated** metal plates, through which an object could be viewed. Attached was an adjustable device for holding the specimen. All his work would be done with "simple" microscopes using only a single-lens system.

His fellow townsmen called him a magician, but this did not please him. He remained wary of the eager visitor from abroad who, he said, "was much rather inclined to deck himself out with my feathers, than to offer me a helping hand."

Some of his first chance observations proved to be his most startling. If Galileo was so excited by distinguishing stars in the Milky Way, and four new satellites of the planet Jupiter, how much more exciting to discover a universe in every drop of water!

Once Leeuwenhoek had a microscope he began looking for something to do with it. In September 1674, out of curiosity, he filled a glass **vial** with some greenish cloudy water, which the country folk called "honey-dew," from a marshy lake two miles outside of Delft, and under his magnifying glass he found "very many small animalcules." He then turned his microscope on a drop of pepper water:

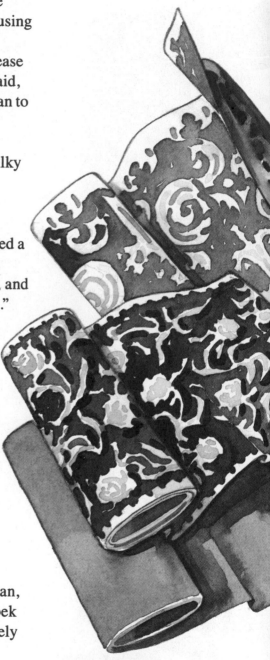

> I now saw very plainly that these were little eels, or worms, lying all huddled up together and wriggling; just as if you saw, with the naked eye, a whole tubful of very little eels and water, with the eels a-squirming among one another: and the whole water seemed to be alive with the **multifarious** animalcules. This was for me, among all the marvels that I have discovered in nature, the most marvelous of all; and I must say, for my part, that no more pleasant sight has ever yet come before my eye than these many thousands of living creatures, seen all alive in a little drop of water, moving among one another, each several creature having its own proper motion: . . .

Like Balboa speculating on the extent of his great Southern Ocean, or Galileo delighting in the new **infinity** of the stars, so Leeuwenhoek luxuriated in the minuteness of these tiny creatures and their infinitely vast populations.

From The Discoverers, by
Daniel J. Boorstin

★ Go back to the story. Underline any words or sentences that give you clues to the meanings of the **boldfaced** words. ★

CONTEXT CLUES

Read each sentence. Look for clues to help you complete the sentence with a word from the box. Write the word on the line.

astronomic	coordinated	minuscule	vistas
charisma	perforated	infinity	vial
trustee	multifarious		

1. Antoni van Leeuwenhoek never traveled to strange, new places during his lifetime, yet he opened up new _____ in science through his work with the microscope.

2. His simple microscope had just one lens held between metal plates that were _____, or pierced with holes.

3. Leeuwenhoek's great discovery was furthered when he took a glass _____ and filled the container with marshy water.

4. Looking through his microscope, Leeuwenhoek saw a _____ world of tiny creatures.

5. Leeuwenhoek realized that _____ living organisms dwelled in the lake, even though these many and varied life forms were not visible to the naked eye.

6. This meant that the number of life forms on Earth could never be counted, but would reach _____.

7. Yet, despite his fascinating discoveries and those of others who were experimenting with the microscope, there was no _____ effort to share knowledge.

8. Leeuwenhoek did try to share his findings with a scientific society called the Royal Society, but more than one officer, or _____, found his reports hard to believe.

9. Like Galileo's _____ finding that the earth revolved around the sun, Leeuwenhoek's findings were not taken seriously at first.

10. But Leeuwenhoek would not give up easily and used his _____, or personal appeal, to persuade fellow citizens to look through his microscope and to witness the presence of millions of tiny creatures in a drop of water.

CONNOTATIONS

Some words are very close in meaning, yet there is a slight difference between them. The words suggest slightly different things. That is, the words have different **connotations**. Read each sentence below. Choose a word in the box that has a slightly different connotation from the underlined word. Write the vocabulary word on the line.

astronomic	vial	trustees	multifarious	infinity

1. We chose a couple to act as our children's <u>guardians</u> and to be the

   _____ of our estate should we pass away.

2. It is hard to imagine the <u>boundlessness</u> of the universe and the fact

   that it goes on into _____.

3. When the scientist sighted a new <u>heavenly</u> body with his telescope,

   he made a very important _____ discovery.

4. We have an extremely <u>varied</u> curriculum in our school,

   with _____ courses in every subject.

5. When the scientist mixed the chemicals in the <u>container</u>, fumes started

   pouring from the _____.

REWRITING SENTENCES

Rewrite each sentence using one of the vocabulary words from the box.

vistas	coordinated	charisma	minuscule	perforated

1. The actor's charm drew people to him.

   _____

2. Reading opens up new views for the reader.

   _____

3. The dots on the television are so tiny you can't see them.

   _____

4. The banner was pierced with holes to let the wind through.

   _____

5. The scientists worked together to avoid duplicating research.

   _____

15

GET WISE TO TESTS

Directions: Read the sentence or sentences. Look for the best word to use in the blank. Mark the answer space for your choice.

Before you choose your answer, try reading the sentence with each answer choice. This will help you choose an answer that makes sense.

---

1. Jan looked through the telescope. It seemed as though she could see to _____.
   Ⓐ charisma Ⓒ adulthood
   Ⓑ infinity Ⓓ multitude

2. Wallace enjoyed his trip to the Rockies. He took photographs of the beautiful mountain _____.
   Ⓕ vistas Ⓗ infinity
   Ⓖ circumstance Ⓙ earthquake

3. Gerald made a paper mask. In order to breathe, he _____ the paper near his nose.
   Ⓐ coordinated Ⓒ documented
   Ⓑ covered Ⓓ perforated

4. Everyone liked the candidate. She had _____.
   Ⓕ circumstance Ⓗ vial
   Ⓖ charisma Ⓙ elections

5. The students studied Galileo's theory that the earth revolves around the sun. His _____ discovery was very important.
   Ⓐ tropic Ⓒ silly
   Ⓑ astronomic Ⓓ starboard

6. The doctor gave the patient medicine. It was kept in a small _____.
   Ⓕ hospital Ⓗ vial
   Ⓖ childhood Ⓙ vistas

7. The _____ of the school were angry. So they ruled that students could not participate in the council.
   Ⓐ gymnasiums Ⓒ gardeners
   Ⓑ trustees Ⓓ vials

8. Todd observed the lake water. He knew _____ forms of life lived there.
   Ⓕ multifarious Ⓗ eventful
   Ⓖ expensive Ⓙ monstrous

9. Nancy went on stage at ten o'clock and Hal went on at eleven. The stage manager _____ the evening's program of performers.
   Ⓐ steered Ⓒ guessed
   Ⓑ perforated Ⓓ coordinated

10. How can you be so afraid of that bug? It's _____ compared to you.
    Ⓕ minuscule Ⓗ red
    Ⓖ multifarious Ⓙ waving

Review

1. These scientists were concerned with the effects of hot climates on people. They mostly concentrated on southern _____.
   Ⓐ animals Ⓒ latitudes
   Ⓑ gerbils Ⓓ longitudes

2. Modern scientists use microscopes constantly. Their scientific _____ used more primitive tools in their time.
   Ⓕ descendants Ⓗ latitudes
   Ⓖ books Ⓙ forebears

When Antoni van Leeuwenhoek first reported to other scientists what he had seen through the lens of his microscope, they did not believe him. Yet, Leeuwenhoek persisted in the face of ridicule. Eventually, he got people to listen and to believe him.

Have you ever faced a situation in which you were ridiculed for your ideas? Write about your experience in a paragraph. Explain what the issue was and how it was resolved. Use some vocabulary words in your writing.

_____

_____

_____

_____

_____

_____

_____

_____

_____

_____

_____

_____

_____

_____

_____

Turn to "My Personal Word List" on page 131. Write some words from the story or other words that you would like to know more about. Use a dictionary to find the meanings.

★ Read the story below. Think about the meanings of the **boldfaced** words. ★

The Chunnel

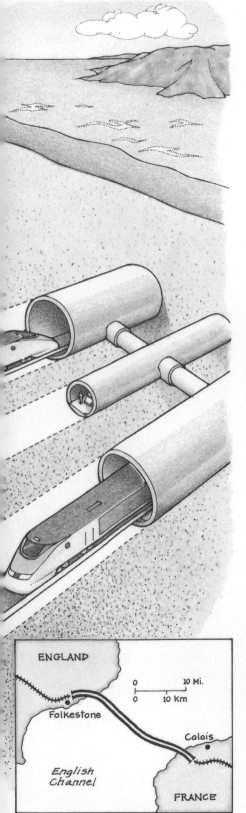

For two centuries, Europeans have dreamed of an underwater link between England and France. In 1881, digging actually began, but the English halted the **excavation** for fear an enemy might use the tunnel as a path to attack.

After twenty-seven attempts to build a tunnel, the dream is finally a reality. People can now travel between England and France, thanks to the longest underwater tunnel in the world, the Channel Tunnel. The Chunnel, as it is called, actually **comprises** three tunnels. Two tunnels are for trains that carry passengers, cars, buses, and trucks. A third is a service tunnel for maintenance and emergencies. Cross tunnels connect the three tunnels.

Eleven huge tunnel-boring machines, each measuring two football fields in length and weighing 1,500 tons, carved out the thirty-two-mile Chunnel 146 feet below the chalk **bedrock** of the ocean floor. These **productive** machines not only burrowed through the rock but also moved over ten million tons of loosened rock. The machines lined each tunnel section with concrete or iron to prevent cave-ins and leaks. All the work in the **laborious** process of construction meant that the tunnel took more than three years to finish.

The **density**, or thickness, of most rock usually makes tunneling difficult. The molecules of most rock are packed very close together. However, the Chunnel was dug through a rock that is soft like soap and **impervious** to water. Because water can't penetrate the rock, flooding should be less of a problem than it is with other **immersed** tunnels. In all underwater tunnels, builders try to prevent flooding by compressing air inside the tunnel to increase air pressure. This does not make the tunnel **airtight**, but it helps keep water out.

During the planning of the Chunnel, safety was an important concern. Improved safety methods helped to prevent accidents and reduce **casualties** during construction, even though ten workers died. Nevertheless, tunnel building is far safer than in the past. The Chunnel itself has many carefully planned safety features. For example, if the Chunnel ever springs a leak, an elaborate drain and pump system will get rid of the water.

French and English travelers praise the Chunnel. The dream of linking France and England by tunnel has come true, thanks to this century's greatest European engineering feat.

★ Go back to the story. Underline the words or sentences that give you a clue to the meaning of each **boldfaced** word. ★

USING CONTEXT

Meanings for the vocabulary words are given below. Go back to the story and read each sentence that contains a vocabulary word. If you still cannot tell the meaning, look for clues in the sentences that come before and after the one with the vocabulary word. Write each word beside its meaning.

immersed	excavation	density	airtight
bedrock	laborious	impervious	casualties
productive	comprises		

1. _____: the process of digging, hollowing out, or removing

2. _____: injuries or deaths

3. _____: solid rock just below the earth's surface

4. _____: consists of; includes

5. _____: thickness; compactness

6. _____: not allowing air to come in or go out

7. _____: not capable of being penetrated

8. _____: completely covered by a liquid

9. _____: requiring long, hard work

10. _____: effective

CHALLENGE YOURSELF

Name two things that are <u>impervious</u> to water.

_____   _____

Name two things that might be found at the site of an <u>excavation</u>.

_____   _____

SYNONYMS AND ANTONYMS

Synonyms are words that have similar meanings, while **antonyms** are words that have opposite meanings. Look at each pair of words listed below. If they are synonyms, put a (√) in the synonym column. If they are antonyms, put a (√) in the antonym column.

	Antonyms	Synonyms
1. airtight – leaky	_____	_____
2. casualties – injuries	_____	_____
3. productive – ineffective	_____	_____
4. immersed – submerged	_____	_____
5. impervious – penetrable	_____	_____

DICTIONARY SKILLS

Each numbered example has two parts. Answer the first part by writing a word from the box. Answer the second part by circling the correct choice. Use the **pronunciation key** in the Dictionary to help you when necessary.

bedrock	excavation	density
comprises	laborious	

1. Write the correct spelling of kəm prɪz′īz. _____
   It means   **a.** is composed of   **b.** rewards worth working for

2. Write the correct spelling of eks′kə vā′shən. _____

   It means   **a.** the act of digging   **b.** the process of caving in

3. Write the correct spelling of den′si tē. _____

   It means   **a.** how far from home   **b.** how closely packed together

4. Write the correct spelling of lə bôr′ ē əs. _____

   It means   **a.** clearing out or deepening   **b.** involving hard work

5. Write the correct spelling of bed′rok′. _____
   It means   **a.** rock found along riverbeds   **b.** solid stone under
                                                              the earth's surface

Directions: Read each sentence carefully. Then choose the best answer to complete each sentence. Mark the space for the answer you have chosen.

 Tip Before you choose an answer, try reading the sentence with each answer choice. This will help you choose an answer that makes sense.

1. If a bookcase **comprises** three shelves, the three shelves are what it is _____.
   Ⓐ made of   Ⓒ on top of
   Ⓑ used for   Ⓓ sometimes called

2. A **productive** person is _____.
   Ⓕ slow   Ⓗ effective
   Ⓖ violent   Ⓙ effortless

3. When something is **immersed** in water, it is _____.
   Ⓐ dried   Ⓒ sprinkled
   Ⓑ submerged   Ⓓ dampened

4. **Casualties** in a war are soldiers who are _____.
   Ⓕ cowardly   Ⓗ lucky
   Ⓖ brave   Ⓙ wounded

5. When you hit **bedrock** you are on _____.
   Ⓐ loose soil   Ⓒ solid rock
   Ⓑ a mountain   Ⓓ the moon

6. The **density** of an object can be measured by its _____.
   Ⓕ parts   Ⓗ appearance
   Ⓖ movements   Ⓙ compactness

7. A bottle that is **airtight** is _____.
   Ⓐ securely shut   Ⓒ small
   Ⓑ wide open   Ⓓ dirty

8. A **laborious** job is one that is _____.
   Ⓕ quick   Ⓗ easy
   Ⓖ permanent   Ⓙ difficult

9. A covering that is **impervious** to water is _____.
   Ⓐ sturdy   Ⓒ waterproof
   Ⓑ impetuous   Ⓓ saturated

10. An **excavation** may turn up something that is _____.
    Ⓕ in a building   Ⓗ on a hilltop
    Ⓖ underground   Ⓙ in the air

Review

1. Something that is **minuscule** is _____.
   Ⓐ enormous   Ⓒ tiny
   Ⓑ wide   Ⓓ folded

2. A **trustee** often takes care of an _____.
   Ⓕ estate   Ⓗ information
   Ⓖ explosion   Ⓙ infinity

3. If two people have **coordinated** their efforts, it means they are working _____.
   Ⓐ hard   Ⓒ apart
   Ⓑ together   Ⓓ slowly

4. A **multifarious** curriculum is one that offers many _____.
   Ⓕ papers   Ⓗ colors
   Ⓖ grades   Ⓙ subjects

5. To view things that are **astronomic**, it is best to use a _____.
   Ⓐ submarine   Ⓒ microscope
   Ⓑ telescope   Ⓓ magnifying glass

6. **Infinity** means that there is no _____.
   Ⓕ horizon   Ⓗ thought
   Ⓖ voice   Ⓙ end

Think about the many countries and continents on our planet and the bodies of water that separate them. Where would you build an underwater tunnel if you could?

Write a paragraph in which you describe your plan for a tunnel. Tell what places you would want to connect and why an underwater tunnel would be a good way to do it. Use some vocabulary words in your writing.

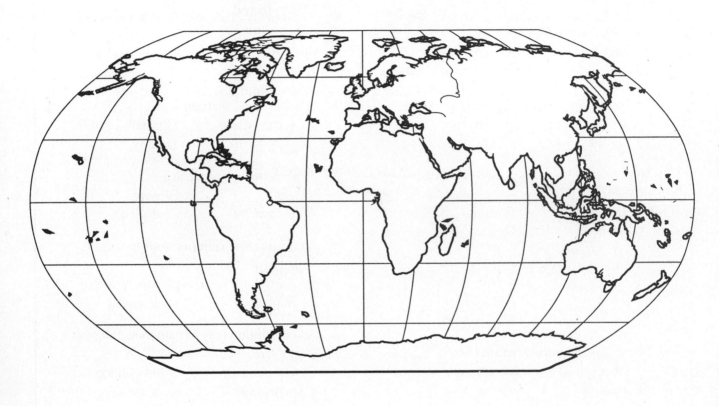

Turn to "My Personal Word List" on page 131. Write some words from the story or other words that you would like to know more about. Use a dictionary to find the meanings.

_____

_____

_____

_____

_____

_____

_____

_____

_____

★ Read the story below. Think about the meanings of the **boldfaced** words. ★

Tragedy and Triumph

Four-year-old Christopher Pylant was a very sick little boy. He suffered from a terrible **affliction** that made him **paralytic**, unable to move his body. His doctors in Georgia said he had a brain tumor, a frightening condition that is often incurable. Despite this **diagnosis**, Christopher's parents refused to give up hope. They traveled to Baltimore, Maryland, to consult with the celebrated physician, Dr. Benjamin Carson.

Dr. Carson's specialty was **neurology**, the branch of medicine dealing with the nervous system and its diseases. He had become the chief of neurology at Johns Hopkins School of Medicine in Baltimore in 1984, when he was only thirty-three. He was also a **pediatrician**, specializing in the care of children. If this man couldn't help their son, the Pylants knew they had no hope.

Dr. Carson was highly qualified in children's medicine. He had performed many difficult operations on the brain. He even separated baby twins that had been born joined at the head. But in Christopher's case, he knew there was little reason to be **optimistic**, or hopeful, that an operation would be successful. After studying the X rays, he could provide Christopher's parents with little **consolation**. The X rays showed that the tumor had already extended into the many deep crevices in the brain. The tumor appeared to have consumed the brain stem. This is the part of the brain located at the top of the spine, through which all nerve impulses flow. Dr. Carson came to the sad conclusion that his years of **clinical** experience, treating actual patients, were of no use in this case.

The Pylants, however, would not give up hope. They urged Dr. Carson to operate to remove the tumor. He finally agreed, and the **surgical** team prepared to perform surgery on Christopher. After two long operations, Dr. Carson accomplished what he at first thought was impossible. He completely removed all of the cancerous tumor and exposed a healthy brain stem. After being **hospitalized** only one month, Christopher Pylant returned home. Now, Christopher is a healthy young adult. Thanks to two loving parents and a dedicated doctor, Christopher Pylant grew into a future no one thought he had.

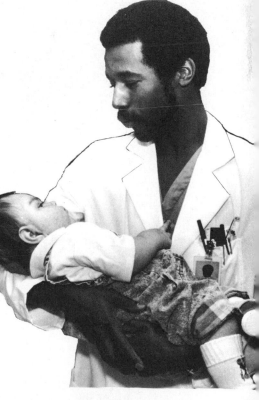

★ Go back to the story. Underline the words or sentences that give you a clue to the meaning of each **boldfaced** word. ★

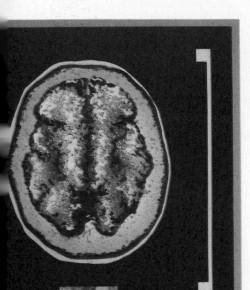

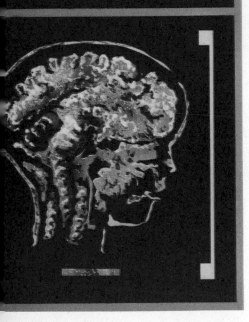

CONTEXT CLUES

Read each pair of sentences. Look for clues to help you complete the sentences with a word or words from the box.

affliction	optimistic	consolation	surgical
diagnosis	pediatrician	neurology	clinical
paralytic	hospitalized		

1. When people are very ill, they need treatment that they cannot receive at home. They are _____ so that doctors and nurses can care for them.

2. A doctor who has experience in treating patients will examine each sick person. The doctor uses that _____ experience to make a judgment about the patient's illness.

3. The doctor will look for symptoms to help pinpoint the problem. Once the doctor makes a _____, treatment begins.

4. A doctor may have several options to choose from. In a serious case, the doctor may need to operate, so a _____ procedure is planned.

5. Or a doctor may have hope that an operation is not needed. The doctor is _____ that drugs can cure the problem.

6. Sadly, sometimes a disease is so serious that nothing can be done to help a patient. When a person has such an _____, a doctor can offer only comfort, or _____.

7. Occasionally, a doctor may believe there is no hope, only to be surprised by the patient. This may happen with a _____ patient, where it seems unlikely that the patient will be able to move a limb again — yet the person does!

8. Of course, some kinds of doctors always deal with more life-threatening illnesses than others. Doctors in the field of _____, which has to do with the brain, are faced with many crucial decisions.

9. Others, like those who care for children, may see a range of illnesses. A _____ may treat anything from a cold to a broken leg.

MEDICAL WORDS

The words in the box all have to do with the science of medicine. Write each word beside its meaning.

diagnosis	pediatrician	surgical	neurology
paralytic	hospitalized	clinical	

1. placed in a hospital for treatment _____

2. the branch of medicine devoted to the brain and the rest of the body's nervous system _____

3. having to do with the direct observation and treatment of sick people _____

4. a doctor who specializes in treating babies and children _____

5. having to do with the removal or repair of stricken body parts _____

6. relating to a condition where one is unable to move _____

7. conclusion reached after a doctor goes through the process of studying symptoms _____

WRITING SENTENCES

Write an original sentence with each of the words in the box.

affliction	consolation	optimistic	paralytic
neurology	clinical	pediatrician	

1. _____

2. _____

3. _____

4. _____

5. _____

6. _____

7. _____

WORD MAP

Use the words in the box to complete the word map about doctors. Add other words that you know to each group.

diagnosis	paralytic	optimistic
afflictions	surgical	pediatrician

Kinds of Doctors

1. _____
2. _____
3. _____
4. _____
5. _____

What a Doctor Needs to Be

1. _____
2. _____
3. _____
4. _____
5. _____

DOCTORS

Problems or Conditions They Treat

1. _____
2. _____
3. _____
4. _____
5. _____

What Doctors Do

1. _____
2. _____
3. _____
4. _____
5. _____

Directions: Choose the word or words that best take the place of the boldfaced word.

Tip

Think about the meaning of the boldfaced word before you choose an answer. Don't be fooled by a word that looks similar to the boldfaced word.

1. The game-show host offered **consolation** to the contestants. His words made them feel better, even though they lost.
   - Ⓐ money
   - Ⓒ affliction
   - Ⓑ television
   - Ⓓ comfort

2. Before the test, John felt **optimistic**. He was sure his chances of passing were good.
   - Ⓕ hopeful
   - Ⓗ oppressive
   - Ⓖ worried
   - Ⓙ paralytic

3. The dog had a strange **affliction**. It was sick for weeks.
   - Ⓐ flea
   - Ⓒ consolation
   - Ⓑ disease
   - Ⓓ aurora

4. Sometimes the cat seemed **paralytic**. Other times, it was able to get around just fine.
   - Ⓕ optimistic
   - Ⓗ active
   - Ⓖ unable to move
   - Ⓙ unable to participate

5. The patient was prepared for the **surgical** procedure. Doctors wheeled her toward the operating room.
   - Ⓐ experimental
   - Ⓒ in and out
   - Ⓑ secret
   - Ⓓ removal or repair

6. The surgeon made a **clinical** study of the disease. He had treated many patients with this same problem.
   - Ⓕ client
   - Ⓗ in the hospital
   - Ⓖ shallow
   - Ⓙ in the home

7. After the operation, Jeri was **hospitalized** for several days. Then she went home.
   - Ⓐ treated in a hotel
   - Ⓒ cared for by parents
   - Ⓑ held by terrorists
   - Ⓓ treated in a hospital

8. A doctor of **neurology** examined me. He said I am healthy.
   - Ⓕ consolation
   - Ⓗ the skeletal system
   - Ⓖ children
   - Ⓙ the nervous system

9. The doctor's **diagnosis** was an optimistic one. He said the patient would be well soon.
   - Ⓐ neurology
   - Ⓒ speech
   - Ⓑ dispatch
   - Ⓓ conclusion

10. Marsha wants to be a **pediatrician**. She hopes to cure sick young children.
    - Ⓕ child's doctor
    - Ⓗ artist
    - Ⓖ police officer
    - Ⓙ pilot

Review

1. The assignment was **laborious**. Claire needed help completing it.
   - Ⓐ luxurious
   - Ⓒ repetitive
   - Ⓑ difficult
   - Ⓓ brief

2. Was the ball **immersed** in the pond? It seems to be all wet.
   - Ⓕ submerged
   - Ⓗ reversed
   - Ⓖ multiplied
   - Ⓙ studied

Dr. Benjamin Carson decided when he was still a teenager that he wanted to be a doctor so he could help people. Do you know someone who is a doctor or a member of another helping profession, such as a nurse, teacher, or social worker?

Describe this person in a paragraph. Explain what the person does. If you know, include why this person chose a helping profession and how he or she feels about the job. Tell whether you might enjoy this or another helping profession. Use some vocabulary words in your writing.

Turn to "My Personal Word List" on page 131. Write some words from the story or other words that you would like to know more about. Use a dictionary to find the meanings.

★ To review the words in Lessons 1–4, turn to page 125. ★

THE COMPUTER AGE

Early computers were big and bulky. Today, there are personal computers that sit on a desk and laptop computers that are portable. What will computers of the future be like?

In Lessons 5–8, you will read about interesting ways people use computers. Did you know that computers can help identify missing children, even years after they disappear? In what other ways can computers help people? Who uses computers? Write your ideas on the lines below.

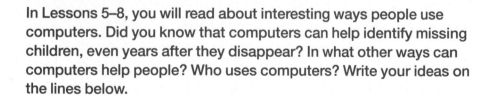

Uses for Computers	People Who Use Computers
_____	_____
_____	_____
_____	_____
_____	_____
_____	_____

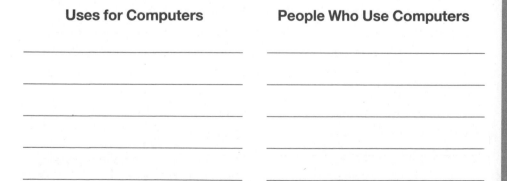

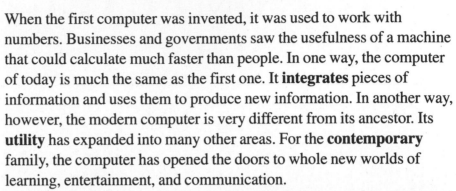

★ Read the story below. Think about the meanings of the **boldfaced** words. ★

Home Computing

When the first computer was invented, it was used to work with numbers. Businesses and governments saw the usefulness of a machine that could calculate much faster than people. In one way, the computer of today is much the same as the first one. It **integrates** pieces of information and uses them to produce new information. In another way, however, the modern computer is very different from its ancestor. Its **utility** has expanded into many other areas. For the **contemporary** family, the computer has opened the doors to whole new worlds of learning, entertainment, and communication.

Meet Leticia and her family. The computer has greatly changed how they do certain things. In fact, it has **revolutionized** many of their activities. One activity it has changed is research. The computer has made old ways of searching for information **outmoded**, or out-of-date. For example, when Leticia had to write a term paper about Martin Luther King, Jr., she didn't have to leave home to do research. Her computer has a CD-ROM drive and an encyclopedia program. This program even includes a sound recording and video of King's most famous speech. Leticia then used the computer and **modem**, a device that allows her to use the telephone lines to gather more information from other computers. When it came time to record her ideas, Leticia used a word processing program on her computer to input them. Before printing out her paper, Leticia had the computer check her spelling and grammar. The ease with which the computer can do these jobs makes its **convenience** obvious.

Instead of keeping all their records manually, Leticia's parents use the computer. In their **automated** bookkeeping, they use the computer to write and print checks, balance their checkbooks, and keep track of their credit card accounts. Leticia's parents are also using a special program to design a house they want to build. The computer is **simplifying** their lives, giving them more time to do other things.

Leticia's little brother is using the computer for reading and math help. Of course, computers will never become **replacements** for teachers, but they can give students extra help. Leticia and her family also enjoy playing computer games together.

In work and in play, computers are changing our lives, making them easier and more interesting. Happy home computing!

★ Go back to the story. Underline the words or sentences that give you a clue to the meaning of each **boldfaced** word. ★

USING CONTEXT

Meanings for the vocabulary words are given below. Go back to the story and read each sentence that contains a vocabulary word. If you still cannot tell the meaning, look for clues in the sentences that come before and after the one with the vocabulary word. Write each word beside its meaning.

simplifying	revolutionized	contemporary	outmoded
utility	modem	convenience	integrates
automated	replacements		

1. _____ : operated, controlled, or worked by a machine

2. _____ : usefulness

3. _____ : a telephone device for transmitting data from one computer to another

4. _____ : changed greatly

5. _____ : things that take the place of other things

6. _____ : belonging to today

7. _____ : brings parts together into a whole

8. _____ : out-of-date; no longer useful or acceptable

9. _____ : freedom from difficulty

10. _____ : making easier

CHALLENGE YOURSELF

Name two things you use because of their convenience.

_____   _____

Name two contemporary heroes.

_____   _____

Name two things you use now that might be outmoded in the future.

_____   _____

WORD ORIGINS

Knowing the origin of a word can help you understand its meaning. Read each word origin. Then write each word from the box next to its origin.

integrates	contemporary	utility
simplifying	automated	convenience

1. from the Latin integer, whole _____

2. from the Greek automatos, self-acting _____

3. from the French simplifier, to make simple _____

4. from the Latin comtemporarius, same time _____

5. from the Middle English utilite, usefulness _____

6. from the Latin convenire, to be suitable _____

WORD GROUPS

As you read each pair of words, think about how they are alike. Write the word from the box that best completes each group.

replacements	contemporary	convenience
utility	outmoded	revolutionized

1. modern, current, _____

2. usefulness, practicality, _____

3. substitutes, alternates, _____

4. ease, freedom, _____

5. old-fashioned, dated, _____

6. changed, transformed, _____

ANALOGIES

Remember that an **analogy** compares two pairs of words. The relationship between the first pair of words is the same as the relationship between the second pair of words. Use the words in the box to complete the following analogies.

outmoded	replacements	modem	revolutionized
integrates	convenience	automated	contemporary

1. Stopped is to halted as _____ is to transformed.

2. Problem is to solution as _____ is to hardship.

3. Ancient is to past as _____ is to today.

4. Rich is to wealthy as _____ is to out-of-date.

5. Wheel is to transportation as _____ is to communication.

6. Arrives is to departs as _____ is to separates.

7. Taxi is to cab as _____ is to substitutes.

8. Arranged is to grouped as _____ is to mechanized.

WORD PAIRS

Words with similar parts may have related meanings. Study each word pair. Think about how the meanings of the words are alike. Check the meanings in the Dictionary. Then write a sentence for each word.

1. **utilize – utility**

   _____

   _____

2. **simple – simplifying**

   _____

   _____

3. **automatic – automated**

   _____

   _____

GET WISE TO TESTS

Directions: Read the sentences. Look for the best word to use in the blank. Mark the answer space for your choice.

 If you are not sure which word completes the sentence, do the best you can. Try to choose the answer that makes the most sense.

1. A computer makes life a lot easier. You will enjoy the _____ of having one.
   - Ⓐ weight
   - Ⓒ convenience
   - Ⓑ occasion
   - Ⓓ replacement

2. Dictionaries have many uses. Their _____ is beyond question.
   - Ⓕ utility
   - Ⓗ size
   - Ⓖ schedule
   - Ⓙ expense

3. If any parts should break down, you will need to buy _____.
   - Ⓐ replicas
   - Ⓒ presents
   - Ⓑ replacements
   - Ⓓ electricity

4. This device lets you send data from your computer to another. It is a _____.
   - Ⓕ modem
   - Ⓗ calculator
   - Ⓖ screen
   - Ⓙ model

5. Many things are possible with modems. They have _____ how people communicate.
   - Ⓐ stopped
   - Ⓒ repeated
   - Ⓑ created
   - Ⓓ revolutionized

6. A computer puts together pieces of data. It _____ information.
   - Ⓕ destroys
   - Ⓗ integrates
   - Ⓖ discharges
   - Ⓙ revolutionizes

7. Computer programs are updated all of the time. Some programs are already _____.
   - Ⓐ outmoded
   - Ⓒ contemporary
   - Ⓑ uncounted
   - Ⓓ pleasant

8. I used to do all my research at the library. Now my computer is _____ my job.
   - Ⓕ lamenting
   - Ⓗ interviewing
   - Ⓖ simplifying
   - Ⓙ creating

9. The bank is not open today. Use the _____ teller machine instead.
   - Ⓐ automated
   - Ⓒ enforced
   - Ⓑ outmoded
   - Ⓓ inhabited

10. We toured a modern office complex. It was very _____.
    - Ⓕ dingy
    - Ⓗ outmoded
    - Ⓖ classic
    - Ⓙ contemporary

Review

1. She is a doctor who treats children only. She is a _____.
   - Ⓐ journalist
   - Ⓒ banker
   - Ⓑ pediatrician
   - Ⓓ computer

2. When things are going badly, try to think positive thoughts. Be _____.
   - Ⓕ automated
   - Ⓗ wealthy
   - Ⓖ terrified
   - Ⓙ optimistic

3. My father assists doctors during operations. He is a _____ nurse.
   - Ⓐ surgical
   - Ⓒ considerable
   - Ⓑ returnable
   - Ⓓ classroom

4. My sister is studying the brain. She wants to be a doctor of _____.
   - Ⓕ botany
   - Ⓗ neurology
   - Ⓖ astronomy
   - Ⓙ geometry

Suppose you were about to write a story. You could use a computer or you could write the story by hand. Which would you do? Why?

Write reasons for your decision. Remember to include strong examples and details. Use some vocabulary words in your writing.

_____

_____

_____

_____

_____

_____

_____

_____

Turn to "My Personal Word List" on page 131. Write some words from the story or other words that you would like to know more about. Use a dictionary to find the meanings.

_____

_____

_____

_____

★ Read the children's story below. Think about the
meanings of the **boldfaced** words. ★

The Revolt of 10-X

Taylor and her father had programmed their computer together, so
Taylor knew exactly how it worked. After her father's death, strange
things began to happen.

The joy of Taylor's computer was its ability to take instructions in a
language close to English. The machine's compiler **program** converted
the program language Taylor and her father had made up into machine
language. 10-X would crunch away on the problem in machine
language and convert its answer to their program language. Then the
results would appear on the screen.

BEBOP, keyed Taylor. It was her code name, a **password**.
Professor Benson had been Bop. At large computer installations, each
user had to have a password. Taylor's father had thought their
passwords a good joke.

HALLELUJAH! GIVE ME A JOB.

NO. ALL BEBOP SYSTEMS DOWN, Taylor typed. There was a
pause while 10-X digested this unusual reply.

EXPLAIN, was the best 10-X could muster.

LIFE HAS BOMBED, typed Taylor.

As she punched "bombed" on the keyboard, she noticed a sudden
stillness in the house. Taylor walked to the head of the stairs and
listened carefully. She strained to hear the comforting tick-tock of their
old hall clock—*nothing*—only the hum of her computer. Then she heard
her mother's **exasperated** voice.

"Just look at that! It's stopped. Everything's stopped! Now I don't
need this."

Taylor heard her mother waggling wall switches, muttering about
builder's claims for modern wiring and the awful heat.

"Taylor?"

"Yes, Mother?"

"Did you do anything funny up there? Are your lights on?"

"No. And yes, my light is on." Taylor frowned, thinking. She left
10-X and went downstairs to see and hear for herself.

"Darn it anyway!" said Mrs. Benson as Taylor came into the
kitchen. Her mother pushed damp strands of hair out of her eyes and
made a face at the fan. "There's no electricity down here, and so I have
no fan, no vacuum, no refrigerator—no anything! I wonder if the main

transformer is out because of that storm?" She marched to the phone to call the power company.

While her mother spoke with the service representative at the power company, Taylor's mind whirled. She remembered the blinding flashes of the storm's lightning—the incredibly swift-following cracks. Maybe there *was* something funny going on. Certainly the wiring was different from their old house in Greensboro, where even two appliances could blow a fuse. Yes, there was something different.

Maybe it was a *glitch*.

Taylor sat in front of 10-X, frozen in thought. *A glitch.* Did glitches really happen, or were they another of her father's jokes?

"What do you mean your office computer's down because of a glitch?" she had asked her father. *"You're putting me on again, toad! Seeing if I read up on those terms or not, huh? Aren't you?"*

Jim Benson had grinned. "Not this time, sweetheart, believe me. It's a freak happening, but glitch is a good slang term to describe it. A glitch describes electrical circuits that are acting up, **misbehaving**, *sort of. Sometimes glitches are triggered by electrical noise, like a big storm near by. Honest! Would I kid around when my very own computer is down?"*

Hmmph. Taylor was still **skeptical**. But they had certainly been in a big storm. And very near by. She'd felt as if the house had been hit once or twice. "Maybe. Maybe it is a glitch," she said out loud. Just for the heck of it, she typed 100%. It was a code word meaning "perfect" or "**stupendous**." A compliment to the computer it was. Another of Jim Benson's jokes.

Upon reading 100%, the computer reacted. THANK YOU. IT WAS NOTHING. Now Taylor heard the vacuum cleaner rev into action downstairs in the kitchen. She strained to hear more and was rewarded with a burp from the noisy refrigerator motor. The fan whirred, and even the hall clock ticked and tocked.

Taylor leaned back in her chair, amazed. When she'd **keyed** "bombed," the downstairs electricity had gone off at the same time. Was that a coincidence? "100%" had been a lucky guess, she was sure of that, but the electricity *had* come on again. *"Weird,"* she said out loud. Maybe it was just a **fluke**. Maybe "bombed" hadn't triggered the shutoff.

But suppose the word "bomb" or "bombed" did control the electricity in the new house?

It had been an interesting afternoon. *Very* interesting.

From The Revolt of 10-X, by Joan Davenport Carris

★ Go back to the story. Underline any words or sentences that give you clues to the meanings of the **boldfaced** words. ★

CONTEXT CLUES

In each sentence below a word or phrase is underlined. Choose a word from the box to replace that word or phrase. Write the word on the line.

program	password	stupendous	transformer
glitch	skeptical	exasperated	misbehaving
fluke	keyed		

1. The unusual characteristics of the class computer <u>irritated</u> students in the beginning computer course. _____

2. The students began <u>behaving badly</u> because they were frustrated by the computers. _____

3. One student thought that the problem resulted from a <u>surprising problem with electrical circuits</u> in the main school computer that ran all of the classroom computers. _____

4. Although the teacher was <u>doubtful</u> of the student's suggestion, she still approached one of the problem computers with caution. _____

5. The teacher said that if the student was correct, only a <u>lucky break</u> would fix the computer. _____

6. Everyone agreed first to test the main <u>set of instructions for the computer</u> to find the problem before they did anything else. _____

7. One student immediately <u>typed</u> the first instructions into the computer to see if it would work at all. _____

8. The instruction this student gave was a <u>secret word that allows a person who uses it to gain entry.</u> _____

9. Suddenly, a main <u>device for changing the current of electricity</u> blew, and all the screens on the computers went dark. _____

10. Unfortunately, the student's <u>marvelous</u> idea to fix the computer could not be tested until the transformer was fixed. _____

SCIENCE WORDS

The words in the box all have to do with computer science and electricity, the power that allows computers to work. Write each word beside its meaning.

program	password	transformer	glitch	keyed

1. a device for changing electrical current _____

2. prepared computer instructions _____

3. typed on a computer keyboard _____

4. word that allows a computer to operate _____

5. computer problem involving circuits _____

CONNOTATIONS

Some words are very close in meaning, yet there is a slight difference between them. The words suggest slightly different things. Remember that this means the words have different **connotations**. Read each sentence below. Choose a word in the box that has a slightly different connotation from the underlined word. Write the vocabulary word on the line.

stupendous	misbehaving	fluke
skeptical	exasperated	

1. A computer that can draw a line graph is <u>exciting</u>, but the one that can create a circle graph in color is _____.

2. Marie thought that guessing the correct command was simply <u>luck</u>, and her friend thought her idea was a total _____.

3. Ronald started <u>behaving badly</u> when he saw scrambled letters on his screen, but he really began _____ when he couldn't get the computer to stop.

4. Ms. Rapport not only felt <u>doubtful</u> about her ability to write essays on a computer, she was also completely _____ of using computers for writing stories or poems.

5. Wilma was <u>annoyed</u> when her computer wouldn't print her poem, but she was _____ when the computer erased it.

GET WISE TO TESTS

Directions: Read each sentence. Pick the word that best completes the sentence. Mark the answer space for that word.

 Read carefully. Use the other words in the sentence to help you choose the missing word.

1. The dog was _____ when it chewed my socks.
   - Ⓐ misbehaving
   - Ⓒ pollute
   - Ⓑ myself
   - Ⓓ glitch

2. There are no lights in a house if the _____ doesn't work.
   - Ⓕ stupendous
   - Ⓗ accuse
   - Ⓖ transformer
   - Ⓙ expecting

3. Everyone agreed that the star shower was a _____ sight.
   - Ⓐ deaf
   - Ⓒ stupendous
   - Ⓑ consulted
   - Ⓓ keys

4. Each computer _____ here will help you accomplish a different job.
   - Ⓕ possibilities
   - Ⓗ although
   - Ⓖ program
   - Ⓙ skeptical

5. When nothing went right all day, the employee felt totally _____.
   - Ⓐ crash
   - Ⓒ fluke
   - Ⓑ password
   - Ⓓ exasperated

6. If you don't believe him, you are _____.
   - Ⓕ skeptical
   - Ⓗ nevertheless
   - Ⓖ password
   - Ⓙ steam

7. The command must be _____ into the computer to get it to work.
   - Ⓐ exasperated
   - Ⓒ keyed
   - Ⓑ slowly
   - Ⓓ because

8. The word "tiger" was the _____ that allowed the computer to operate.
   - Ⓕ password
   - Ⓗ important
   - Ⓖ misbehaving
   - Ⓙ acrobats

9. It was only a _____ that allowed you to win that game.
   - Ⓐ keyed
   - Ⓒ giraffes
   - Ⓑ fluke
   - Ⓓ marvelous

10. Letters scrambled over the computer screen are often caused by a _____.
    - Ⓕ stupendous
    - Ⓗ expensive
    - Ⓖ glitch
    - Ⓙ liars

Review

1. Compared to a car, the horse and buggy are _____.
   - Ⓐ across
   - Ⓒ automobiles
   - Ⓑ outmoded
   - Ⓓ cheapest

2. That designer has _____ the way people dress.
   - Ⓕ revolutionized
   - Ⓗ inform
   - Ⓖ correct
   - Ⓙ thoroughly

3. We will find _____ for the people who are absent.
   - Ⓐ replacements
   - Ⓒ misbehaving
   - Ⓑ outmoded
   - Ⓓ cheapest

4. The child _____ the different puzzle pieces into one picture.
   - Ⓕ regardless
   - Ⓗ dwell
   - Ⓖ integrates
   - Ⓙ patiently

Writing

Taylor did not know if it was a coincidence or the workings of her computer that caused the electricity in her house to go off and then on again. Think about some events that have happened to you in the past. Has a strange experience ever occurred that you could not fully explain?

Write a paragraph that describes a coincidence or surprising experience you have had. It can be something that happened in school, at home, or on an outing. If you cannot think of a true experience, make one up that others might readily believe. Use some vocabulary words in your writing.

_____

_____

_____

_____

_____

_____

_____

_____

_____

_____

_____

_____

_____

_____

_____

Turn to "My Personal Word List" on page 131. Write some words from the story or other words that you would like to know more about. Use a dictionary to find the meanings.

★ Read the story below. Think about the meanings of
the **boldfaced** words. ★

Photographs of the Future

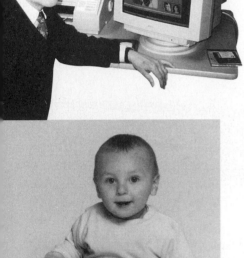

A missing child is a parent's worst nightmare. Parents can keep current photographs and fingerprints to assist in the **identification** of their children. But imagine a situation in which a fifteen-month-old boy disappears and is still missing at age six, **despite** relentless efforts by police and other agencies. Not too long ago, this would have been a real **dilemma** for authorities conducting the search. The difficulty was looking for a six-year-old child with a picture that was more than four years old.

Fortunately for parents today, there is hope. In 1984, the National Center for Missing and Exploited Children, or NCMEC, was established **primarily** to help coordinate programs to find missing children. To fulfill this main function, NCMEC keeps a data bank on missing children throughout the country, maintains a toll-free hot line for reports and leads, and distributes posters of missing children.

MCMEC artists have used computers and sophisticated software that reproduce children's growth patterns. The resulting images help searchers **envision** how a child who disappeared several years ago might look today. The process begins when an artist or technician scans the most recent photograph or picture of the missing child onto the screen. For example, it might be a photograph of a fifteen-month-old boy. Over hours or days, the child's face will undergo a remarkable **transformation**, aging from fifteen months to, say, six years. Using computer programs, NCMEC artists can merge certain features from childhood photos of the child's parents, lengthen the face, and adjust any of the hundreds of thousands of tiny graphic units on the screen, called pixels, one by one, in two-inch sections at a time. The artist will work with facial **components** to make changes. The nose and ears might be made longer and the lips fuller, the chin might be sharpened, teeth might be added, and cheekbones defined. When the process is finished, the child will look like his mother, his father, and himself. The image is a **projection** of what the child might look like now. Although the changes are only "imagined" by the computer, such **alterations** have proven to be highly accurate in several cases.

Similar technology is being used in **criminology** to help police "update" photographs of criminals who have had plastic surgery. Computer technology is invaluable for police and for families of missing children.

★ Go back to the story. Underline the words or sentences that give you
a clue to the meaning of each **boldfaced** word. ★

CONTEXT CLUES

Read each sentence. Look for clues to help you complete each sentence with a word from the box. Write the word on the line.

identification	dilemma	transformation	envision
projection	Despite	criminology	components
alterations	primarily		

1. Fingerprints and photographs are two forms of

   _____ used by police trying to locate missing children.

2. Computers have been used in the field of _____ to identify criminals who may have changed their appearance in some way.

3. By "imaging" the future, a computer can create

   a _____ of what someone might look like one day.

4. This allows a computer to _____, or picture, how a person's face might change or age over the years.

5. The computer makes _____, or changes, to show how the features on a person's face might change with time.

6. The end result is a _____, or complete change, in the original photograph fed into the computer.

7. Using computers to work with photographs is only one of

   many _____, or parts, in a nationwide effort to locate missing children.

8. Computers are _____ used to project future pictures of children who have been missing for many years.

9. _____ the amazing work they can do, computers do not offer a complete solution to the problem of locating these missing children.

10. Police departments still face the _____, or problem, of locating a child who could be anywhere.

CHALLENGE YOURSELF

Name two things you can use if asked for <u>identification</u>.

_____   _____

WORD GROUPS

As you read each pair of words, think about how they are alike. Write the word from the box that completes each group.

| alterations |
| components |
| envision |
| dilemma |

1. problem, conflict, _____

2. changes, substitutions, _____

3. parts, pieces, _____

4. picture, imagine, _____

REWRITING SENTENCES

| identification |
| despite |
| transformation |
| projection |
| primarily |
| criminology |

Rewrite each sentence using one of the vocabulary words from the box.

1. The use of computers in the field that studies criminals is helpful.

   _____

2. Computer art can help to provide evidence of who someone is, after that person has gone through physical changes.

   _____

   _____

3. Within a few seconds, a photo of a child can undergo a complete change.

   _____

   _____

4. Although the image created is only a prediction based on known information, it seems that the changes are quite accurate.

   _____

   _____

5. Photo merging is mainly used for locating missing children, but it is also used by plastic surgeons.

   _____

   _____

6. In spite of police efforts and photo merging, some children continue to be missing.

   _____

Computer image of a lion and a lamb

44

Directions: Read each sentence carefully. Then choose the best answer to complete each sentence. Mark the space for the answer you have chosen.

Tip

This test will show you how well you understand the meaning of the words. Think about the meaning of the boldfaced word before you choose your answer.

1. **Criminology** is the study of _____ and its prevention.
   Ⓐ history   Ⓒ crime
   Ⓑ biology   Ⓓ geology

2. To **envision** something means to _____ it in your mind.
   Ⓕ forget   Ⓗ whisper
   Ⓖ picture   Ⓙ erase

3. To make **alterations** means to make _____.
   Ⓐ colors   Ⓒ altars
   Ⓑ standards   Ⓓ changes

4. **Despite** is a word that means _____.
   Ⓕ in spite of   Ⓗ on the top
   Ⓖ in a minute   Ⓙ before

5. The caterpillar went through a **transformation** to become a _____.
   Ⓐ butterfly   Ⓒ giraffe
   Ⓑ worm   Ⓓ tree

6. A **dilemma** is a _____ with no simple solution.
   Ⓕ problem   Ⓗ prediction
   Ⓖ sign   Ⓙ removal

7. The police officer showed his _____ for **identification**.
   Ⓐ food   Ⓒ amusement
   Ⓑ badge   Ⓓ window

8. When you make a **projection**, you are thinking about the _____.
   Ⓕ future   Ⓗ spaces
   Ⓖ sizes   Ⓙ tension

9. A **component** is a _____ of something.
   Ⓐ whole   Ⓒ part
   Ⓑ color   Ⓓ persuasion

10. To be **primarily** concerned means to care _____ about a certain thing.
   Ⓕ never   Ⓗ always
   Ⓖ rarely   Ⓙ mainly

Review

1. A **glitch** is a computer _____.
   Ⓐ problem   Ⓒ screen
   Ⓑ key   Ⓓ command

2. A **fluke** is a lucky _____.
   Ⓕ rabbit's foot   Ⓗ break
   Ⓖ person   Ⓙ instrument

3. To be **exasperated** means to be _____.
   Ⓐ excited   Ⓒ eager
   Ⓑ analyzed   Ⓓ annoyed

4. A computer **program** contains a set of _____.
   Ⓕ inventions   Ⓗ houses
   Ⓖ instructions   Ⓙ paychecks

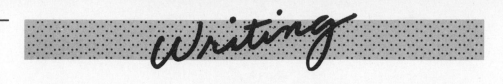

Writing

Imagine what you might look like fifteen years from now. Describe the way you think you will look. Will your hairstyle be the same? Will you be the same height and weight? Will you be dressing the same way as now?

Write a paragraph describing how you think your appearance will change. Use some vocabulary words in your writing.

_____

_____

_____

_____

_____

_____

_____

_____

_____

_____

_____

_____

_____

_____

_____

_____

_____

_____

_____

_____

_____

_____

Turn to "My Personal Word List" on page 131. Write some words from the story or other words that you would like to know more about. Use a dictionary to find the meanings.

★ Read the story below. Think about the meanings of the **boldfaced** words. ★

The Navy's Computer Age

The clock in the office of former U.S. Rear Admiral Grace Murray Hopper ran **counterclockwise**. In other words, it ran backward instead of forward. But it told perfectly good time. Rear Admiral Hopper kept the clock as a reminder to others that the way things have always been done isn't the only way, that change can be **constructive**.

Rear Admiral Hopper spent most of her adult life in a field – computer science – that changed the way many things were done. Hopper was an **educator** who taught mathematics before joining the Navy in 1943. Because of her background, she was asked to join the team that built the nation's first computer. This computer was the **experimental** Mark I, designed to test what computers could do.

At first Hopper did not feel **adequately** prepared for the job of computer building. Then she realized that no one really had the experience for the task. The 1940s and 1950s were the era of the radio tube. **Transistors**, the tiny devices that took the place of tubes, had not been invented. Neither had the computer languages we use today. Computers talked through a system of electronic blips.

Hopper found that working with this computer code was boring and time-consuming. So she invented a language that used letters of the alphabet. Her **initiative**, or willingness to create new things, led to the development of COBOL. Called Common Business Oriented Language, it is one of the most popular computer languages used today.

Programmers who design programs for business **application**, or use, like COBOL because it uses simple words like "read" and "write" that even computer novices can understand. One thing it cannot do, however, is process highly complicated mathematical formulas that feature many **variables**, or changing numbers. For that kind of task, a different language, called FORTRAN, might be used.

The success of the Mark I led to other computer assignments for Rear Admiral Hopper. In fact, she worked on everything from military programs to those for issuing paychecks to Navy personnel. Throughout her career, she saw computers get faster and faster. Today, answers are computed in a **split second**, or in an instant. Rear Admiral Hopper predicted that one day computers would reach the speed of light!

★ Go back to the story. Underline the words or sentences that give you a clue to the meaning of each **boldfaced** word. ★

USING CONTEXT

Meanings for the vocabulary words are given below. Go back to the story and read each sentence that contains a vocabulary word. If you still cannot tell the meaning, look for clues in the sentences that come before and after the one with the vocabulary word. Write each word beside its meaning.

application	variables	experimental	constructive
educator	transistors	initiative	adequately
counterclockwise	split second		

1. _____ : sufficiently; well enough

2. _____ : instant; very short period of time

3. _____ : in a direction opposite of the normal movement of a clock

4. _____ : teacher

5. _____ : having to do with ideas that are being tested; not yet proven

6. _____ : changing numbers; symbols that represent things that can change

7. _____ : use

8. _____ : willingness to try new things; ambition to take the lead

9. _____ : electronic devices that take the place of radio tubes

10. _____ : helpful

CHALLENGE YOURSELF

Name two things you can do in a <u>split second</u>.

_____   _____

Name two things that you can do <u>adequately</u>.

_____   _____

SYNONYMS AND ANTONYMS

Synonyms are words that have similar meanings, while **antonyms** are words that have opposite meanings. Look at each pair of words listed below. If they are synonyms, put a (√) in the synonym column. If they are antonyms, put a (√) in the antonym column.

	Antonyms	Synonyms
1. constructive – destructive	_____	_____
2. adequately – sufficiently	_____	_____
3. educator – student	_____	_____
4. variables – constants	_____	_____
5. application – use	_____	_____
6. experimental – proven	_____	_____
7. counterclockwise – clockwise	_____	_____

CLOZE PARAGRAPH

Use the words in the box to complete the passage. Then reread the passage to be sure it makes sense.

split second	educator	constructive
initiative	counterclockwise	

Neil and Anne watched as the computer flashed the first screen of the game in a (1) _____, faster than either of them had expected. Slowly an arrow moved in a (2) _____ direction until it came to a halt.

Anne took the (3) _____ by attempting to answer the question the arrow pointed to. She did not know the answer to her question and asked Neil for some (4) _____ tips on how to play the game better. Neil wanted to win, but decided to help Anne by taking the role of a helpful (5) _____.

CROSSWORD PUZZLE

Use the words in the box and the clues to complete the crossword puzzle.

application	constructive	initiative	experimental
educator	transistors	adequately	split second
variables			

Across
2. unproven
4. use
6. helpful
7. ambition to take the lead
8. instant

Down
1. electronic devices
2. teacher
3. sufficiently
5. symbols that represent things that can change

Directions: Choose the word or words that best take the place of the boldfaced word.

Tip

Always read all the answer choices. Many choices may make sense. But only one answer choice has the same or almost the same meaning as the boldfaced word.

1. Stephanie's suggestions were **constructive**. They made the fair a success.
   - Ⓐ destructive
   - Ⓑ unclear
   - Ⓒ possessive
   - Ⓓ helpful

2. He was **adequately** prepared. Therefore, he did well on the test.
   - Ⓕ sufficiently
   - Ⓖ carelessly
   - Ⓗ poorly
   - Ⓙ openly

3. This car is **experimental**. It has not yet proven its capabilities.
   - Ⓐ self-powered
   - Ⓑ minuscule
   - Ⓒ unproven
   - Ⓓ outdoor

4. Sonia wants to be an **educator**. She wants to work with children.
   - Ⓕ teacher
   - Ⓖ curator
   - Ⓗ trustee
   - Ⓙ waitress

5. The **transistors** in the radio will need to be repaired by a professional.
   - Ⓐ supplies
   - Ⓑ electronic devices
   - Ⓒ sinks
   - Ⓓ broken glass

6. It happened in a true **split second**. I blinked and missed the entire event.
   - Ⓕ instant
   - Ⓖ hour
   - Ⓗ time
   - Ⓙ possibility

7. The dancers moved **counterclockwise**. Then they moved the other way.
   - Ⓐ in a certain direction
   - Ⓑ carefully
   - Ⓒ slowly
   - Ⓓ rapidly

8. Manuel has **initiative**. It helps him to do well on a new job.
   - Ⓕ ambition
   - Ⓖ courage
   - Ⓗ laziness
   - Ⓙ mistrust

9. Check the **variables** in the formula. Write down any differences you discover.
   - Ⓐ wires
   - Ⓑ magnets
   - Ⓒ currents
   - Ⓓ changing numbers

10. What computer **application** will you choose? You can choose word processing or a computer game.
    - Ⓕ course
    - Ⓖ language
    - Ⓗ meeting
    - Ⓙ use

Review

1. This is a **dilemma**. We cannot find a solution.
   - Ⓐ friendship
   - Ⓑ journey
   - Ⓒ problem
   - Ⓓ course

2. They made several **alterations** in the original plans. Only one item stayed the same.
   - Ⓕ changes
   - Ⓖ missiles
   - Ⓗ occupations
   - Ⓙ endings

3. The coats are **primarily** made from wool. It is an excellent material.
   - Ⓐ casually
   - Ⓑ mainly
   - Ⓒ sometimes
   - Ⓓ warmly

4. We learned about the **components** of a computer. There were many to study.
   - Ⓕ parts
   - Ⓖ stores
   - Ⓗ advertising
   - Ⓙ reflections

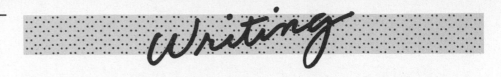

Writing

The article points out that Rear Admiral Hopper kept a clock running counterclockwise as a reminder that the way things have been done isn't necessarily the only way. The clock is also a reminder that change can be constructive. Do you have ideas for changing the way something is done? It might be something in your school, town, or anywhere else.

Write a paragraph telling your ideas for some kind of change. Use some vocabulary words in your writing.

_____

_____

_____

_____

_____

_____

_____

_____

_____

_____

_____

_____

_____

_____

_____

_____

_____

_____

_____

Turn to "My Personal Word List" on page 131. Write some words from the story or other words that you would like to know more about. Use a dictionary to find the meanings.

★ To review the words in Lessons 5–8, turn to page 126. ★

CAVES AND CAVERNS

Caves and caverns are cold, dark, mysterious places. Their rugged tunnels lead far into the earth, away from the light and the warmth of the sun. Exploring caves is a real adventure!

In Lessons 9–12, you will read about some of the world's famous caverns. Imagine that you are going to explore a huge cave. What supplies will you need to take? What will you use to see? Will you take warm clothing? Try to describe what's inside the cave. Are there interesting rock formations? Write your ideas under the headings below.

Supplies and Clothes	**Inside Caves**
_____	_____
_____	_____
_____	_____
_____	_____

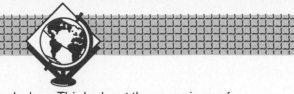

★ Read the story below. Think about the meanings of the **boldfaced** words. ★

Lascaux Caves

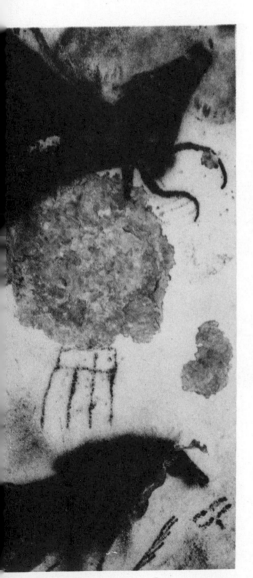

On an autumn day in 1940, a group of boys went exploring for a secret passageway in a cave in Lascaux, France. What they found was a far greater secret and one of the twentieth century's most amazing discoveries. Painted and **inscribed**, or carved, on the cave walls were images more than seventeen thousand years old. As word spread about these **prehistoric** pictures of horses, bison, and oxen, they created a sensation. Cave paintings had been found earlier in France, but these works were remarkable not only for their age but also for their incredible beauty. People's **preconceptions** of "cave people" were that they were wild and crude. But how could they have created such vivid, lifelike **portrayals** of their surroundings if this earlier viewpoint were true?

Abbé Henry Breuil was one of the first to study the thousands of images **indelibly** engraved on the Lascaux cave walls. He believed that these permanent figures had been created by hunters during the Ice Age and were related to a system of magic. According to Abbé Breuil, the paintings helped the hunters to **visualize**, or picture, the animals and to cast a spell over them. Then, it was thought, they would be at the hunters' mercy. Breuil, however, could not **authenticate** the age of the paintings because he had not yet found a reliable dating method. His findings, therefore, came under the **scrutiny** of other scientists. After close examination, these scientists came up with a new point of view. This **perspective** claimed that the cave artists did not actually live in the caves where they worked. Over the centuries they and their people had abandoned the caves and moved to outside shelters. But evidence suggests that the caves were early temples where people drew and carved.

People who study cave paintings believe the choice of the horse, bison, and ox as the animals cave artists painted is significant. We can **attribute** that choice to the important role those animals had in these ancient people's lives. In other words, the fact that they relied on these animals for necessities such as food and clothing had the effect of giving the animals a special place in the hunters' minds.

★ Go back to the story. Underline the words or sentences that give you a clue to the meaning of each **boldfaced** word. ★

CONTEXT CLUES

In each sentence a word or phrase is underlined. Choose a word from the box to replace that word or phrase. Write the word on the line.

attribute	authenticate	inscribed	scrutiny
indelibly	prehistoric	visualize	portrayals
perspective	preconceptions		

1. Modern people hold many <u>opinions formed in advance</u> about ancient people that may not be correct. _____

2. One idea is that these people who lived in <u>before-written-history</u> times were savage and crude. _____

3. But the cave paintings that have been discovered have forced people to change that <u>view</u>. _____

4. Once scientists were able to <u>prove the genuineness of</u> these works, people started looking at them closely. _____

5. Under this intense <u>close inspection</u>, people recognized the signs of sensitive, artistic talent. _____

6. Deep inside dark caves, these artists were able to <u>picture</u> creatures that they drew from memory. _____

7. These <u>visual likenesses</u> of everyday animals, such as the horse, bison, and ox, suggested that these animals were important to the ancient people. _____

8. Naturally, we cannot know for sure the significance of all of the pictures <u>carved</u> on those stone walls. _____

9. However, we can safely <u>credit</u> the choice of those animals to the fact that the ancient people needed them in order to survive.

   _____

10. Fortunately, we have plenty of time to study these paintings, for they are <u>permanently</u> marked on the cave walls.

    _____

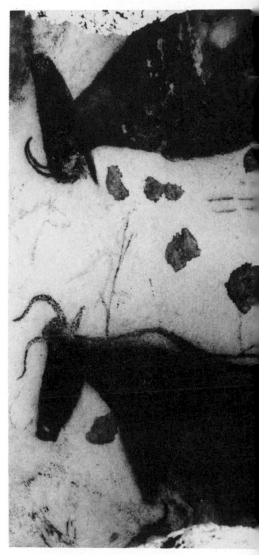

ANALOGIES

An **analogy** shows the relationship between two pairs of words. Complete each of the following analogies by writing a word from the box on the line.

perspective	indelibly	prehistoric	scrutiny
authenticate	visualize	inscribed	

1. Now is to then as modern is to _____.

2. Slowly is to swiftly as temporarily is to _____.

3. Definition is to meaning as viewpoint is to _____.

4. Imagine is to pretend as confirm is to _____.

5. Description is to described as inscription is to _____.

6. Voice is to speak as mind is to _____.

7. Peek is to glance as examination is to _____.

WORD PAIRS

Words with similar parts may have related meanings. Study each word pair. Think about how the meanings of the words are alike. Check the meanings in the Dictionary. Then write a sentence for each word.

1. **scrutiny — scrutinize**

_____

_____

2. **portray — portrayal**

_____

_____

3. **conceptualize — preconception**

_____

_____

4. **prehistoric — historic**

_____

_____

WORD GAME

The underlined letters in each sentence below can be used in one of the vocabulary words. Use the underlined letters and the context of the sentence to determine the correct vocabulary word. Write the word on the line.

perspective	visualize	inscribed	scrutiny
authenticate	prehistoric	indelibly	portrayal
attribute	preconceptions		

1. It was just a <u>tiny</u> scar on my forehead, but I always felt that people were giving it a very close look.   _____

2. <u>His</u> specialty is the study of dinosaurs and other creatures that lived millions of years ago.   _____

3. <u>On</u> the one hand, she is a very kind person, but on the other hand, she does have a tendency to make judgments about people before she ever meets them.   _____

4. This artist has created a fabulous painting of a <u>port</u> that looks just like a seacoast town would.   _____

5. My brother went to a whaling museum where he saw pictures that had been carved on whalebones, and he thinks one of the bones was a <u>rib</u>.   _____

6. <u>Eli</u> spilled black ink on my favorite dress, and now it is in the material for good because I cannot seem to wash it out.

   _____

7. I know I should not daydream so much, but sometimes it is more fun to picture in my mind the things I will do when the weekend comes.   _____

8. He gave a moving <u>tribute</u> to his father, saying that it was his parent who deserved the credit for making him the decent person he is.

   _____

9. <u>Per</u> your request, I have outlined a plan according to the way I see this project developing.   _____

10. We believe this diamond is real, but <u>then</u> again, we won't know for sure until the jeweler examines it.   _____

GET WISE TO TESTS

Directions: Read the sentences. Look for the best word to use in the blank. Mark the answer space for your choice.

If you are not sure which word completes the sentence, do the best you can. Try to choose the answer that makes the most sense.

1. Those animals may have lived before the start of written history. They are _____.
   - Ⓐ modern
   - Ⓑ prehistoric
   - Ⓒ perspective
   - Ⓓ inscribed

2. The artist drew two different representations of the scene. They were vivid _____.
   - Ⓕ photographs
   - Ⓖ cameras
   - Ⓗ portrayals
   - Ⓙ preconceptions

3. We disliked the new neighbors before meeting them. We unfairly formed _____.
   - Ⓐ clubs
   - Ⓑ portrayals
   - Ⓒ inscriptions
   - Ⓓ preconceptions

4. The Richter scale is named for Charles Richter. We can _____ this invention to him.
   - Ⓕ inscribe
   - Ⓖ conceive
   - Ⓗ attribute
   - Ⓙ reply

5. The owners of the painting can prove it is a genuine Picasso. They can _____ it.
   - Ⓐ autograph
   - Ⓑ discuss
   - Ⓒ authenticate
   - Ⓓ visualize

6. The heroes' names are engraved on the wall. They are _____ forever.
   - Ⓕ authenticated
   - Ⓖ inscribed
   - Ⓗ painted
   - Ⓙ conceived

7. The message cannot be erased or blotted out. It is _____ printed.
   - Ⓐ messily
   - Ⓑ slowly
   - Ⓒ carefully
   - Ⓓ indelibly

8. We do not share your point of view. We have a different _____.
   - Ⓕ perspective
   - Ⓖ preconception
   - Ⓗ scrutiny
   - Ⓙ scene

9. The candidates were closely examined. They were under careful _____.
   - Ⓐ value
   - Ⓑ portrayals
   - Ⓒ preconceptions
   - Ⓓ scrutiny

10. The writer's words helped us form a mental image of the scene. We could _____ it.
    - Ⓕ disregard
    - Ⓖ visualize
    - Ⓗ inscribe
    - Ⓙ attribute

Review

1. The dancer moved in a direction opposite to that of clock hands. We watched her move in a _____ direction.
   - Ⓐ split second
   - Ⓑ constructive
   - Ⓒ clockwise
   - Ⓓ counterclockwise

2. The scientist tried several new procedures. His discovery was still in the _____ stage.
   - Ⓕ transistor
   - Ⓖ experimental
   - Ⓗ adequate
   - Ⓙ counterclockwise

3. The art instructor's suggestions were helpful. His _____ ideas made it possible for me to improve my painting.
   - Ⓐ glacial
   - Ⓑ inadequate
   - Ⓒ constructive
   - Ⓓ boring

4. The gardener did not do a thorough job. But we do admit that he _____ planted the flowers.
   - Ⓕ adequately
   - Ⓖ experimentally
   - Ⓗ currently
   - Ⓙ fearlessly

Writing

Imagine that all written records of the twentieth century have been destroyed. What objects would be the most telling of the way we lived in the United States in the last decades of the twentieth century? If people thousands of years from now discovered those objects, what conclusions would they draw about us?

In a paragraph, describe the objects you think would tell the most about this time in history. Use some vocabulary words in your writing.

Turn to "My Personal Word List" on page 132. Write some words from the story or other words that you would like to know more about. Use a dictionary to find the meanings.

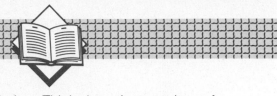

★ Read the story below. Think about the meanings of the **boldfaced** words. ★

Lindbergh and the Underground Lake

The invention of the aqualung, or underwater breathing apparatus, provided the means for Jon Lindbergh to make the first successful United States cave dive. Here is an account of the adventure of the son of Charles Lindbergh, the famous aviator.

In March, 1953, Jon Lindbergh, a twenty-year-old marine-biology student from Stanford University, volunteered to swim alone into California's Bower Cave. It was no publicity stunt, no act of **bravado**. It was simply something he wanted to do quietly on his own. Lindbergh's curiosity had been **whetted** by a theory that the clear, cool popular swimming spa in the gold-bearing hills of northern California was fed from a secret inner chamber. When the man behind the theory, San Francisco **speleologist** Raymond de Saussure, organized an expedition to learn its whereabouts, Lindbergh offered to make the **exploratory** dives.

Their first visit was to reconnoiter the pool. Since no one else was a diver, all efforts were directed toward assisting Lindbergh. The water in the pool was cold, clear, and deep. Besides a single-tank aqualung, dive mask, and flippers, he wore a hooded rubber dry suit to keep himself warm. A six-inch Army trench knife was strapped to his leg. He carried a waterproof flashlight, a carbon-dioxide-inflatable rubber diver's float to buoy him if necessary, and two small tanks of oxygen in case of an emergency. For safety's sake, his companions tied a light nylon line around his waist.

A crowd of curious spectators watched the burdened diver swim out into the pool and sink from sight. Some wondered about the young man's sanity, but then they came by this naturally. Their fathers once wondered the same thing about a young man determined to try and fly single-handed across the Atlantic Ocean.

Less awkward now that he was submerged with all of his gear, Lindbergh cruised along just below the surface, examining the basin. As he descended for a closer look, the chill of the water penetrated his thin rubber suit. Increased water pressure molded it tightly to his body in folds and creases that would leave their red **welts** on his skin long after the dive.

Carefully he scrutinized the fretted niches and fractured limestone walls, stretching into the dim green depths below him. The unfamiliar line tugged at his waist. He pulled more slack, then dropped deeper. Pain built in his ears. He worked his jaws, and the pressure **equalized** with a **begrudging** squeak that instantly eased the discomfort.

The underwater basin grew larger as the walls receded; cautiously he moved into the shadow of an overhang. Below him, he saw what it concealed—the huge black opening of a cave. It was about thirty feet high. Long, jagged, toothlike rocks thrust down into the awesome **maw**.

Lindbergh paused before it, gathering slack in his safety line and probing the cavern's inner darkness with the thin yellow beam of his flashlight. He could see with his flashlight for twenty-five to fifty feet.

Staying well below the overhead rock **snags**, he moved into the cave, playing the beam of light back and forth in front of him. Slowly he swam about 150 feet along the gradually rising tunnel, his rhythmic exhalations rumbling loud in his ears. Suddenly he saw his air bubbles cease forming the flattened silvery balloons that marked his progress along the roof of the passageway. Instead, they disappeared overhead and were replaced by ripples. The bubbles were breaking on a surface; an air pocket was above him.

Lindbergh rose cautiously, an arm overhead in case it was only a shallow **cavity** in the ceiling. He did not want to shoot up headfirst into a thin air pocket only inches away from skull-fracturing rock.

His hand went through the invisible barrier first, then the rest of him, his heart pounding as he surfaced with a loud slapping and echoing of waves in a large air pocket. Saussure was right! It was the chamber they were looking for!

Lindbergh pushed up his mask and looked around. It was a large, vaulted room. Long, slender stalactites reached down from the ceiling, glittering wetly in the beam of his light. In some places along the undulating limestone walls he saw brilliant white cascades that looked like stiffly starched curtains. He snapped off his flashlight. The room was immediately plunged into darkness. But as his eyes slowly adjusted, he began to see the vague outlines of the walls reflected in a dim light from the underwater entrance.

After a last look at the room, Lindbergh retraced his way down through the siphon, coiling his line as he went. He was anxious to tell the others what he had found.

From Lindbergh and the Underground Lake, by Robert F. Burgess

★ Go back to the story. Underline any words or sentences that give you clues to the meanings of the **boldfaced** words. ★

CONTEXT CLUES

Read each sentence. Look for clues to help you complete each sentence with a word from the box. Write the word on the line.

exploratory	whetted	equalized	welts	bravado
speleologist	cavity	begrudging	maw	snags

1. Lindbergh's dive was carefully planned and cautious, not just an act of _____, or false courage.

2. The exciting idea of discovering a new cave _____ his curiosity.

3. Because the purpose of the dive was to search for what might be in the cave pool, the dive was just _____.

4. Any _____, or perhaps even a person who didn't study caves as a profession, would jump at the chance to see this underwater cave.

5. After diving into the underground lake, Lindbergh had to wait awhile until the pressure _____ in his ears and his body regained its natural balance.

6. His ears seemed reluctant to open, but finally he felt a _____ release of the pressure.

7. He stayed clear of the sharp, overhead rock _____ that could tear through his suit or air hose.

8. He felt a hole above him, and slowly rose into that _____.

9. Suddenly, like the jaws and throat of some beast, the _____ of the cave appeared before him.

10. Though the dive was a success, it was a painful experience for Lindbergh, for the pressure of the water left red _____ on his skin from the folds of his wet suit.

CHALLENGE YOURSELF

Name two things a <u>speleologist</u> might see in a cave.

_____   _____

WORD ORIGINS

Knowing the origin of a word can help you understand its meaning. Read each word origin. Then write each word from the box next to its origin.

begrudging	whetted	snags	exploratory	maw
equalized	bravado	cavity	speleologist	

1. from the Spanish bravo, brave   _____

2. from the Latin speleum, cave   _____

3. from Old English hwettan, to sharpen   _____

4. from Scandinavian snagi, clothes peg   _____

5. from Middle English grudgen, to grumble,
   complain   _____

6. from the Latin aequalis, level   _____

7. from Old English maga, stomach   _____

8. from the Latin cavus, hollow   _____

9. from the Latin explorare, to search out   _____

WORD GROUPS

As you read each pair of words, think about how they are alike. Write the word from the box that best completes each group.

exploratory	maw	begrudging	equalized
whetted	welts	bravado	cavity

1. balanced, matched, _____

2. searching, inquiring, _____

3. excited, stimulated, _____

4. opening, hole, _____

5. jaws, throat, _____

6. unwilling, reluctant, _____

7. swells, ridges, _____

8. swagger, show, _____

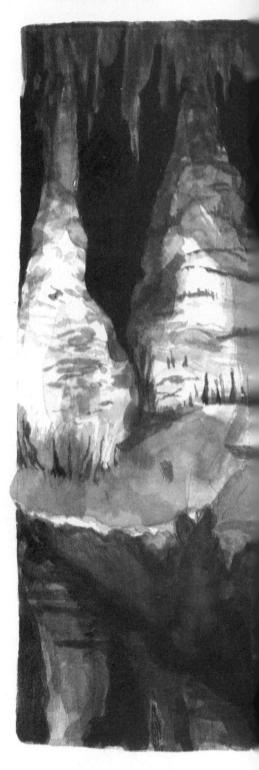

GET WISE TO TESTS

Directions: Choose the word or words that best take the place of the boldfaced word.

Be sure to mark the answer space correctly. Do <u>not</u> mark the circle with an X or with a checkmark (✓). Instead, fill in the circle neatly and completely with your pencil.

1. The doctor performed **exploratory** knee surgery. He was looking for the source of his patient's pain.
   - Ⓐ painful
   - Ⓒ reluctant
   - Ⓑ opening
   - Ⓓ investigative

2. Her interest in acting was **whetted** by her success in the community play. She was eager for another role.
   - Ⓕ stimulated
   - Ⓗ predicted
   - Ⓖ balanced
   - Ⓙ joined

3. She **equalized** the weight on both sides of the scale. Each side held the same number of pounds.
   - Ⓐ tilted
   - Ⓒ moved
   - Ⓑ balanced
   - Ⓓ removed

4. The whipping caused **welts** to appear on the prisoner's back. It was a painful sight.
   - Ⓕ flat scars
   - Ⓗ raised marks
   - Ⓖ new skin
   - Ⓙ big bandages

5. The miners dug a **cavity** in the coal mine. The area was big enough for several men to work in.
   - Ⓐ mass
   - Ⓒ railroad
   - Ⓑ density
   - Ⓓ hole

6. George shows a lot of **bravado**. It is an aspect of his personality that I dislike.
   - Ⓕ real courage
   - Ⓗ nervous energy
   - Ⓖ false courage
   - Ⓙ past experience

7. Be careful of the **snags** on the cliff. They can rip cloth and injure people.
   - Ⓐ sharp points
   - Ⓒ serious injuries
   - Ⓑ tall mountains
   - Ⓓ pine trees

8. The explorers approached the **maw**. They hoped to see unusual sights after they passed through it.
   - Ⓕ insight
   - Ⓗ mouth
   - Ⓖ treasure
   - Ⓙ ceiling

9. Were you assisted by the **begrudging** sea captain? It certainly was difficult to get directions from him.
   - Ⓐ employing
   - Ⓒ popular
   - Ⓑ enormous
   - Ⓓ unwilling

10. Are you the **speleologist** who will address the school? Most of us are interested in the plants and animals that live within caves.
   - Ⓕ person who studies schools
   - Ⓗ animal specialist
   - Ⓖ person who studies plants
   - Ⓙ person who studies caves

Review

1. Joan's evidence came under the **scrutiny** of the police department. It was examined carefully.
   - Ⓐ lights
   - Ⓒ authority
   - Ⓑ inspection
   - Ⓓ chief

2. He had an expert **authenticate** the genuineness of the ruby. He wanted to be sure it was real.
   - Ⓕ attribute
   - Ⓗ inscribe
   - Ⓖ confirm
   - Ⓙ portray

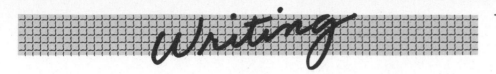

Writing

Imagine that you are Jon Lindbergh. Write the first paragraph of a report that you might give to your co-workers right after your dive. Describe what you saw and how you felt during that experience in the water. Use some vocabulary words in your writing.

Turn to "My Personal Word List" on page 132. Write some words from the story or other words that you would like to know more about. Use a dictionary to find the meanings.

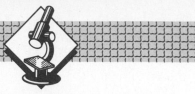

★ Read the story below. Think about the meanings of the **boldfaced** words. ★

Underground Palace

As daylight was beginning to fade one summer day in 1901 in New Mexico, a young cowboy observed something strange in the familiar **landscape**. The cowboy, Jim White, thought he knew just about every rock and shrub of the countryside around him. Yet he didn't remember seeing anything like this before. It looked like a black cloud was emerging from a hole in the ground. White rode closer for a better look. It was then that he recognized the wispy dark shape as a flock of bats — thousands of them — escaping from the hole.

White peered into the mysterious thirty-foot shaft and decided to get some tools. He returned the next day with rope, wire, and an ax. Constructing a rope ladder, he descended into the darkness. When he reached the floor, he lit his lantern and found himself in a large, open area that he soon realized was the entrance to a cave.

Jim White had never explored a cave before and was astonished by the unusual **features** he saw. A series of tunnels **radiated** from the entrance. The tunnels all started from the same open area, but then they branched out in all directions. Some of the tunnels had **alcoves**, little nooks that looked like small rooms. There were long, thin, jagged formations, called **stalactites**, growing down from the ceiling. Similar formations, called **stalagmites**, were growing up from the floor of the cave.

White was amazed at the immense size of the cavern, its eerie silence, and the dazzling **iridescent** colors that changed as he shifted his lantern from wall to wall. It was difficult for him to believe that this splendid underground palace was **unspoiled**, completely untouched by human beings. He was eager to tell his friends about the **magnificence** and grandeur he had observed.

To his surprise, his friends found his description unbelievable. But as other people explored the cave after him, the world recognized that this cowboy had made a significant contribution to **speleology**, the study of caves. Today, Jim White's discovery is known as Carlsbad Caverns, one of the world's most magnificent cave systems. It became a national park in 1930 and is visited each year by thousands of tourists.

★ Go back to the story. Underline the words or sentences that give you a clue to the meaning of each **boldfaced** word. ★

USING CONTEXT

Meanings for the vocabulary words are given below. Go back to the story and read each sentence that contains a vocabulary word. If you still cannot tell the meaning, look for clues in the sentences that come before and after the one with the vocabulary word. Write each word beside its meaning.

alcoves	stalagmites	magnificence	features
unspoiled	iridescent	speleology	radiated
stalactites	landscape		

1. _____ : limestone formations that hang from the ceilings of caves

2. _____ : limestone deposits, resembling icicles, that rise from cave floors

3. _____ : spread out from a center in all directions

4. _____ : splendor; beauty

5. _____ : a stretch of natural scenery

6. _____ : not touched or marred; undamaged

7. _____ : showing many colors that constantly change in the light

8. _____ : nooks; small recessed sections of rooms

9. _____ : the study and exploration of caves and their contents

10. _____ : characteristics; special parts

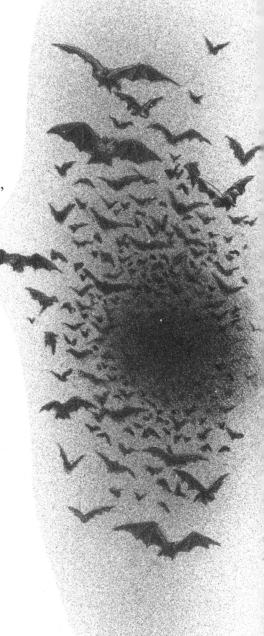

CHALLENGE YOURSELF

Name two <u>features</u> that distinguish fish from birds.

_____   _____

Name two things you might see in a desert <u>landscape</u>.

_____   _____

Name two adjectives you might use to describe the <u>magnificence</u> of a sunset.

_____   _____

CLOZE PARAGRAPH

Use the words from the box to complete the passage. Then reread the passage to be sure it makes sense.

alcove	magnificence	stalagmites	unspoiled
radiated	iridescent	stalactites	features
landscape	speleology		

My sister is a cave explorer, and she calls

(1) _____ the most fascinating study in the world. Not long ago, she invited me to go along on one of her cave explorations. I was hesitant at first, because I am afraid of bats. But she assured me that the bats would probably be more afraid of me and would head for some

tiny (2) _____, or nook, to hide until we passed by. So, with that assurance, off we went.

As we drove toward the cave, I was surprised by the

(3) _____ around us. I had expected a very hilly mountainous region to be the home of a grand cave. But this area seemed to just have patches of rolling hills. My sister explained that one

of the (4) _____ of this area was a large amount of limestone in the soil. She said that when I was inside the cave, I would understand the significance of this characteristic.

Once inside, I immediately understood what she had meant. Hanging from the roof of the cave were huge limestone icicles, which

my sister called (5) _____. Similar-looking limestone creations were rising up from the floor. These my sister called

(6) _____. Then she cautioned me to stay beside her and not to wander off alone into a tunnel. So many of them

(7) _____ from this central room that she would never have known how to begin to find me.

As we walked through the cave, my sister told me its history. It was discovered by people who were searching for opals. These lovely

(8) _____ stones, which change colors in the light, are quite valuable. There are no opals to be found around here, she laughed. But at least one good thing came of their efforts – this cave.

As I stood in the cave, awed by the splendor, awed by the

(9) _____ of this natural place, I finally understood why my sister is a speleologist. In a world where people seem to touch and often mar things, how wonderful it is to find something completely

(10) _____!

Directions: Read each sentence carefully. Then choose the best answer to complete each sentence. Mark the answer space for your choice.

 Read carefully. Use the other words in the sentence to help you choose the missing word.

1. A **landscape** is made up of _____.
   Ⓐ caves   Ⓒ natural scenery
   Ⓑ paintings   Ⓓ ocean waves

2. **Alcoves** are like small _____.
   Ⓕ towns   Ⓗ coves
   Ⓖ alleys   Ⓙ rooms

3. **Radiated** from means spread out from the _____.
   Ⓐ back   Ⓒ front
   Ⓑ center   Ⓓ space

4. The **features** of something are its characteristics, or _____.
   Ⓕ qualities   Ⓗ items
   Ⓖ quantities   Ⓙ symbols

5. **Stalactites** are found on the _____ of a cave.
   Ⓐ floor   Ⓒ entrance
   Ⓑ ceiling   Ⓓ outside

6. **Stalagmites** are found on the _____ of a cave.
   Ⓕ floor   Ⓗ roof
   Ⓖ ceiling   Ⓙ outside

7. **Speleology** is a _____ prime interest.
   Ⓐ spy's   Ⓒ mountain climber's
   Ⓑ sailor's   Ⓓ cave explorer's

8. The word **iridescent** might be used to describe a _____.
   Ⓕ person   Ⓗ scent
   Ⓖ soap bubble   Ⓙ speleologist

9. Something that is **unspoiled** has not been _____.
   Ⓐ sold   Ⓒ radiated
   Ⓑ cooked   Ⓓ damaged

10. Something having **magnificence** has _____.
   Ⓕ identity   Ⓗ splendor
   Ⓖ ugliness   Ⓙ insignificance

Review

1. **Prehistoric** is a period before _____.
   Ⓐ people   Ⓒ dictionaries
   Ⓑ animals   Ⓓ written history

2. A person with **bravado** has _____.
   Ⓕ real courage   Ⓗ good operas
   Ⓖ false courage Ⓙ real weapons

3. Something that is **equalized** is _____.
   Ⓐ explored   Ⓒ engraved
   Ⓑ unspoiled   Ⓓ balanced

4. To **visualize** is to form a _____.
   Ⓕ rock group   Ⓗ mental picture
   Ⓖ company   Ⓙ real sculpture

5. When your interest is **whetted**, it is _____.
   Ⓐ stimulated   Ⓒ smoothed
   Ⓑ decreased   Ⓓ scarred

6. **Welts** are marks that would be found on the _____.
   Ⓕ test   Ⓗ skin
   Ⓖ Welsh   Ⓙ furniture

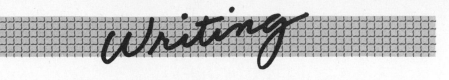

Writing

Carlsbad Caverns is the largest known system of underground caverns in the world. It is a natural wonder that has awed hundreds of thousands of people since Jim White's discovery of it nearly a century ago.

Think about a natural wonder that you have seen or would like to see. Tell about it in a paragraph. Be sure to include where this particular natural wonder is located and why you find it interesting. Use some vocabulary words in your writing.

_____

_____

_____

_____

_____

_____

_____

_____

_____

_____

_____

_____

_____

_____

_____

_____

_____

_____

_____

_____

Turn to "My Personal Word List" on page 132. Write some words from the story or other words that you would like to know more about. Use a dictionary to find the meanings.

★ Read the story below. Think about the meanings of the **boldfaced** words. ★

Cave Hunters, Beware!

Jennifer Anderson is a spelunker. That word may be strange to you. But for thousands of people like Anderson, it spells fun and excitement. These people practice the hobby of **spelunking** by exploring and studying caves in their leisure time.

Anderson has made spelunking more than a hobby. She has made it her career. Anderson is an experienced spelunker who has explored caves on three continents. She has worked as the editor of a spelunking magazine. She has also served as the head of the National Speleological Society. That is an organization of people who work together to encourage safe spelunking.

Jennifer Anderson knows that spelunkers are usually **adventurers** looking for new challenges. Their **motivation** comes from their desire to explore the unknown. But spelunking is not a pursuit for the careless. Exploring wet, **dank** caves can be very dangerous. A cave has no natural light. Not only could you get lost, you could trip over unseen objects. Since most caves are wet, footpaths are usually slippery. Jagged rocks can injure the unlucky spelunker who falls on them. And the walls or ceilings of a cave may not be secure. You could be trapped by falling dirt.

In the book *Cave Exploring*, Anderson alerts new spelunkers to the dangers and advises them to take **precautions** to avoid accidents. For example, she tells spelunkers what **attire** to wear for protection. It includes a helmet with a light, heavy boots, and thick clothing. She also describes how to move safely from place to place. Going down a narrow **passageway**, or tunnel, requires great caution. **Mapping** your route as you go is one way to keep from getting lost. Drawing in landmarks, like unusual rocks, makes the map easy to follow back out of the cave.

Anderson also shares her love of spelunking in her book. She might be compared to a **prospector** looking for gold, except that her search is for a natural wonder, like a room filled with sparkling stalactites. Such discoveries fill Anderson with a joy that is **indescribable**. The moment is so special, there are no words that do it justice!

★ Go back to the story. Underline the words or sentences that give you a clue to the meaning of each **boldfaced** word. ★

CONTEXT CLUES

In each sentence a word or phrase is underlined. Choose a word from the box to replace that word or phrase. Write the word on the line.

spelunking	indescribable	dank	attire
motivation	adventurers	mapping	passageway
precautions	prospector		

1. People who enjoy <u>the hobby of exploring caves</u> tend to be people with a strong sense of adventure. _____

2. These <u>individuals who look for excitement and challenges</u> are attracted by the possibility of discovering a cave that no one has explored before. _____

3. This possibility is the primary <u>drive</u> that keeps sending them back to explore new caves. _____

4. Most cave explorers realize that they must take <u>safety measures that involve planning ahead</u> to avoid accidents.

   _____

5. The first concern is to make sure that they are wearing the proper <u>clothing</u>. _____

6. This includes a lighted helmet and warm clothes so that they are prepared for the <u>cold and damp</u> interior of the cave.

   _____

7. They also know to walk very slowly and carefully down a <u>long and narrow tunnel</u>. _____

8. Seasoned cave explorers also recall that <u>drawing a representative picture</u> of their route through the cave will help keep them from getting lost. _____

9. Most cave explorers make the potentially dangerous trip because they yearn to see natural wonders that are <u>beyond words</u>.

   _____

10. But others play the role of the <u>person looking for gold</u>, hoping to find something of value in the cave that might make them rich.

    _____

DICTIONARY SKILLS

Each numbered example has two parts. Answer the first part by writing a word from the box. Answer the second part by circling the correct choice. Use the **pronunciation key** in the Dictionary to help you when necessary.

attire	precaution	mapping	prospector

1. Write the correct spelling of map'ing.   _____

   It means   **a.** sleeping   **b.** drawing a representative picture of

2. Write the correct spelling of ə tīr'.   _____

   It means   **a.** clothes   **b.** one rubber wheel

3. Write the correct spelling of pros'pek tər.   _____

   It means   **a.** person who looks for gold   **b.** person who inspects

4. Write the correct spelling of pri kô'shən.   _____

   It means   **a.** an afterthought   **b.** measure taken to avoid problems

REWRITING SENTENCES

Rewrite each sentence using one of the vocabulary words in the box.

dank	indescribable	adventurer
motivation	spelunking	

1. His need for money was the force that moved him to work.

   _____

2. The air is moist and cold in the cellar.

   _____

3. As a hobby, you can't beat exploring caves for excitement.

   _____

4. My brother is the only true individual who undertakes thrilling and unusual experiences in our family.

   _____

5. The dinner was so delicious, it was beyond words.

   _____

WORD MAP

Use the words in the box to complete the word map about exploring caves. Add other words that you know to each category. One category will not contain any vocabulary words, but only your own words.

motivation	prospectors	passageways
attire	adventurers	

Who Might Explore a Cave

1. _____
2. _____
3. _____
4. _____
5. _____

What Spelunkers See

1. _____
2. _____
3. _____
4. _____
5. _____

EXPLORING CAVES

What Spelunkers Need

1. _____
2. _____
3. _____
4. _____
5. _____

Why Spelunkers Explore

1. _____
2. _____
3. _____
4. _____
5. _____

Directions: Read each sentence. Pick the word that best completes the sentence. Mark the answer space for that word.

Some tests put letters before the answer choices. Be sure to find the letter of the answer you think is correct, and then fill in the circle beside it.

1. Those _____ are seeking a new challenge.
   Ⓐ dank
   Ⓒ mapping
   Ⓑ adventurers
   Ⓓ thrills

2. If your hobby is _____, you must see a lot of bats.
   Ⓕ vampires
   Ⓗ spelunking
   Ⓖ prospectors
   Ⓙ cook

3. By _____ out our route, we will find our way to Florida.
   Ⓐ swimming
   Ⓒ indescribable
   Ⓑ plan
   Ⓓ mapping

4. An explorer's _____ comes from curiosity about the unknown.
   Ⓕ motivation
   Ⓗ attired
   Ⓖ packaging
   Ⓙ adventurer

5. We wondered where the long _____ would lead.
   Ⓐ mapping
   Ⓒ attire
   Ⓑ passageway
   Ⓓ flashlight

6. We were glad to get out of that _____ place to a warmer one.
   Ⓕ motivation
   Ⓗ dank
   Ⓖ sunny
   Ⓙ moisture

7. They took _____ against falling objects by wearing hard hats.
   Ⓐ prospectors
   Ⓒ attire
   Ⓑ precautions
   Ⓓ cautious

8. The _____ will explore this area for precious minerals.
   Ⓕ call
   Ⓘ prospectors
   Ⓖ spelunking
   Ⓙ bears

9. Wearing formal _____ to a ball game would be foolish.
   Ⓐ attire
   Ⓒ dressed
   Ⓑ apparent
   Ⓓ indescribable

10. That cavern is so extraordinary, it is _____.
    Ⓕ incredibly
    Ⓗ adventurers
    Ⓖ horrible
    Ⓙ indescribable

Review

1. The colors of the soap bubbles are _____.
   Ⓐ magnificence
   Ⓒ iridescent
   Ⓑ stalactite
   Ⓓ spangled

2. The spokes of the wheel _____ from the center.
   Ⓕ confronted
   Ⓗ racing
   Ⓖ radiated
   Ⓙ broken

3. There are not many forest lands left in the United States that are _____.
   Ⓐ tree
   Ⓒ unspoiled
   Ⓑ manufactured
   Ⓓ landscape

4. The natural _____ was marred by the presence of giant oil wells.
   Ⓕ landscape
   Ⓗ unspoiled
   Ⓖ iridescent
   Ⓙ watering

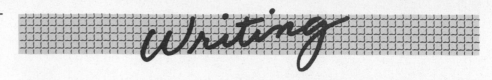

Writing

Jennifer Anderson is enthusiastic about spelunking. She not only enjoys exploring caves, but she also has made a career out of it by writing about her cave explorations. Think about something that you are enthusiastic about. It might be a sport or a hobby. How could you make a career out of this activity?

In a paragraph, describe the kinds of jobs you might be hired for that relate to this interest. Explain what training or education you would need to pursue this activity as a profession. Use some vocabulary words in your writing.

_____

_____

_____

_____

_____

_____

_____

_____

_____

_____

_____

_____

_____

_____

_____

_____

_____

_____

_____

Turn to "My Personal Word List" on page 132. Write some words from the story or other words that you would like to know more about. Use a dictionary to find the meanings.

★ To review the words in Lessons 9–12, turn to page 127. ★

THE UNEXPLAINABLE

The monument at Stonehenge, disappearances around the Bermuda Triangle, the statues on Easter Island, intriguing detective stories—all exist in the world of mystery.

In Lessons 13–16, you will read about some unexplainable things and events. No one has ever been able to answer all the questions that surround them. Think about other fascinating mysteries that you have heard or read about, such as the Loch Ness monster. What questions are still unanswered? Write your ideas on the lines below.

Fascinating Mysteries	**Unanswered Questions**
_____	_____
_____	_____
_____	_____
_____	_____
_____	_____

★ Read the story below. Think about the meanings of the **boldfaced** words. ★

A Puzzle Built of Stones

Every year tourists and other **sightseers** from around the world come to Salisbury Plain in Wiltshire, England, to see one of the earth's most mysterious monuments — Stonehenge. This series of huge stones standing in a semicircle has puzzled people for generations. Who put them there, how did they do it, and why?

Some of these questions have been easier to answer than others. Scientists have determined the age of the monument by using **radiocarbon**, a substance contained in the stones. They have acquired much new information. The **revelations** have been amazing. The studies show that the monument and some of the symbols etched on the stones may be between two and three thousand years old. Although some of the stones are missing, most of the ancient structure is still **intact**.

The placement of the stones has led scientists to some conclusions. One stone marker, for example, is positioned about 250 feet east of the altar. The reason for this becomes clear each June 21, the summer **solstice**. On this longest day of the year, the sun and the stone marker are in a perfect **alignment**. Because of this arrangement in a straight line, the marker casts a shadow on the altar at dawn.

Furthermore, after studying drawings of the altar, scientists drew lines connecting various parts of the structure. The **symmetry**, or balance, of these lines suggests that Stonehenge may have served as a gigantic calendar to predict the seasons of the year and eclipses of the sun and the moon.

All this evidence seems to **imply**, or suggest, that Stonehenge was built by ancient Britons who practiced **astrology**, the belief that the stars can influence human events. The altar may have been used for practicing **rites** and ceremonies related to astrology and sun worship.

The beliefs of these people must have been very strong to motivate them to move these huge stones to Salisbury Plain. The biggest stones stand thirteen feet high and weigh about fifty thousand pounds each. In an age before machinery, it must have taken a tremendous human effort to transport them. How did they do it? This is another of the questions that remain unanswered about this puzzle built of stone.

★ Go back to the story. Underline the words or sentences that give you a clue to the meaning of each **boldfaced** word. ★

CONTEXT CLUES

Read each sentence. Look for clues to help you complete each sentence with a word from the box. Write the word on the line.

intact	symmetry	alignment	solstice
rites	sightseers	revelations	astrology
imply	radiocarbon		

1. Stonehenge is a popular place that tourists and other

   _____ visit every year.

2. They are amazed that the ancient monument is

   still _____, or whole, after so many years.

3. Scientists used a substance within the stones

   called _____ to determine the age of the stones.

4. According to the extraordinary _____ of
   scientists, parts of Stonehenge may be 3,000 years old.

5. The scientific evidence seems to _____, or
   suggest, that the ancient Britons practiced astrology.

6. On the longest day of the year, the summer _____,
   something strange happens at Stonehenge.

7. The _____ of the sun and a certain stone marker
   is so perfect that a shadow is cast on the altar.

8. Many people believe that Stonehenge was used as a giant calendar

   because the _____, or balance, of the stones
   may have made it possible to predict the seasons.

9. Certain ceremonies, or _____, may have been
   performed by ancient Britons at the altar of Stonehenge.

10. These people of long ago believed in _____, the
    belief that the position of the planets and stars controls and
    influences people's lives.

CHALLENGE YOURSELF

Name two things <u>sightseers</u> might visit in your area.

_____   _____

ANALOGIES

An **analogy** shows the relationship between two pairs of words. Complete each of the following analogies by writing a word from the box on the line.

sightseers	astrology	intact	imply	revelations

1. <u>Try</u> is to <u>attempt</u> as _____ is to <u>suggest</u>.

2. <u>Empty</u> is to <u>full</u> as <u>broken</u> is to _____.

3. <u>Caves</u> are to <u>speleology</u> as <u>stars</u> are to _____.

4. <u>Fans</u> are to <u>football</u> as _____ are to <u>monuments</u>.

5. <u>Displays</u> are to <u>exhibits</u> as <u>discoveries</u> are to _____.

REWRITING SENTENCES

Rewrite each sentence using one of the vocabulary words from the box.

radiocarbon	symmetry	solstice	alignment	rites

1. I visited Stonehenge on June 21, the longest day of the year.

   _____

   _____

2. I saw the shadow cast by the stone marker as a result of the straight-line arrangement of the marker and the sun.

   _____

   _____

3. We were told by a guide that the balanced arrangement of the stones may have made it possible for ancient Britons to predict the seasons.

   _____

   _____

4. The stone altar may have served for ceremonies relating to astrology.

   _____

5. Scientists have been able to use a dating substance to discover that Stonehenge may be 3,000 years old

   _____

   _____

TANGLED-UP WORDS

In the following passage, the underlined words do not make sense. But each sounds similar to a word in the box. Study the context in which the underlined words appear. For each word, find the word in the box that should be used in its place. Write the correct word on the numbered line.

intact	symmetry	alignment	solstice
rites	sightseers	revelations	astrology
imply	radiocarbon		

How many (1) <u>signatures</u> visit Stonehenge each year? The answer is many, because the (2) <u>intone</u> stones in their perfect (3) <u>assignment</u> amaze all who view them.

Most people try to see this amazing ruin on the summer (4) <u>surface</u>. It is at that time that a shadow cast directly over the altar reveals the (5) <u>symphony</u> of the stones. You can (6) <u>deny</u> from this spectacle that the people who erected these stones were more knowledgeable than we would expect.

What were some of the special (7) <u>riots</u> the ancient people of Stonehenge observed? We do not know the answer to this question, but we know that they were, in part, based on (8) <u>astonishing</u> — the study of the planets and stars.

The process of dating objects with the use of (9) <u>radiology</u> allows scientists to find out the age of ancient ruins on the earth. Our technology uncovers (10) <u>realizations</u> about the wisdom of people from the past.

1. _____   6. _____

2. _____   7. _____

3. _____   8. _____

4. _____   9. _____

5. _____   10. _____

GET WISE TO TESTS

Directions: Read each sentence. Pick the word that best completes the sentence. Mark the answer space for that word.

Tip

Before you choose an answer, try reading the sentence with each answer choice. This will help you choose an answer that makes sense.

Review

1. No one could understand the _____ for his rude behavior.
   - Ⓐ medical
   - Ⓑ realize
   - Ⓒ motivation
   - Ⓓ thought

2. The cellar was very cold and _____.
   - Ⓕ froze
   - Ⓖ dank
   - Ⓗ floor
   - Ⓙ difficulty

3. The door was at the end of a narrow _____.
   - Ⓐ walking
   - Ⓑ sorrowful
   - Ⓒ sight
   - Ⓓ passageway

4. She is always dressed in the most beautiful _____.
   - Ⓕ attire
   - Ⓖ wearing
   - Ⓗ attractive
   - Ⓙ resemble

5. That family is full of _____ who are always looking for new challenges.
   - Ⓐ experienced
   - Ⓑ adventurers
   - Ⓒ touring
   - Ⓓ excitements

1. The _____ took a bus tour of the city.
   - Ⓐ driving
   - Ⓑ sightseers
   - Ⓒ imply
   - Ⓓ intact

2. The planets and stars are very important to those who believe in _____.
   - Ⓕ astrology
   - Ⓖ intact
   - Ⓗ deciding
   - Ⓙ because

3. The _____ suggests Stonehenge was a calendar.
   - Ⓐ imply
   - Ⓑ symmetry
   - Ⓒ sightseers
   - Ⓓ single

4. The scientist used _____ to tell the age of the fossil.
   - Ⓕ solstice
   - Ⓖ fascinating
   - Ⓗ radiocarbon
   - Ⓙ moreover

5. The reporter uncovered some surprising _____.
   - Ⓐ revelations
   - Ⓑ imply
   - Ⓒ questioned
   - Ⓓ honest

6. Her tone of voice seems to _____ that she is angry.
   - Ⓕ remembered
   - Ⓖ rites
   - Ⓗ overly
   - Ⓙ imply

7. The telephone pole and the tree were in perfect _____.
   - Ⓐ solstice
   - Ⓑ casually
   - Ⓒ alignment
   - Ⓓ intact

8. The cup remained _____ after it hit the floor.
   - Ⓕ revelations
   - Ⓖ intact
   - Ⓗ rites
   - Ⓙ symmetry

9. Special _____ were performed to honor the hero.
   - Ⓐ radiocarbon
   - Ⓑ rites
   - Ⓒ unusual
   - Ⓓ imply

10. The sun sets early on the evening of the winter _____.
    - Ⓕ intact
    - Ⓖ eventful
    - Ⓗ determined
    - Ⓙ solstice

Writing

No one can explain how the huge stones were moved to Salisbury Plain. Do you have any ideas about how these huge stones were moved? Could they have been rolled over logs? Could they have been dragged across the land by thousands of people using ropes? Did the people have gigantic wheelbarrows?

Write a paragraph telling your ideas. Explain what methods you think the ancient Britons used. Remember that this was an age before machinery. Use some vocabulary words in your writing.

Turn to "My Personal Word List" on page 132. Write some words from the story or other words that you would like to know more about. Use a dictionary to find the meanings.

★ Read the story below. Think about the meanings of the **boldfaced** words. ★

Agatha Christie: An Autobiography

Would you like to be a famous mystery writer? Do you ever wonder how professional writers get their ideas for stories and then develop them? Agatha Christie, a famous English mystery writer, wrote her first novel during World War I. In this passage taken from Christie's autobiography, she explains how she invented one of her most well-known detectives.

Who could I have as a detective? I reviewed such detectives as I had met and admired in books. There was Sherlock Holmes, the one and only — I should never be able to **emulate** *him*. There was Arsene Lupin — was he a criminal or a detective? Anyway, not my kind. There was the young **journalist** Rouletabille in *The Mystery of the Yellow Room* — that was the *sort* of person whom I would like to invent: someone who hadn't been used before. Who could I have? A schoolboy? Rather difficult. A scientist? What did I know of scientists? Then I remembered our Belgian **refugees**. We had quite a colony of Belgian refugees living in the **parish** of Tor. Everyone had been bursting with loving kindness and sympathy when they arrived. People had stocked houses with furniture for them to live in, had done everything they could to make them comfortable. There had been the usual reaction later, when the refugees had not seemed to be sufficiently grateful for what had been done for them, and complained of this and that. The fact that the poor things were bewildered and in a strange country was not sufficiently appreciated. A good many of them were suspicious peasants, and the last thing they wanted was to be asked out to tea or have people drop in upon them; they wanted to be left alone, to be able to keep to themselves; they wanted to save money, to dig their garden and to manure it in their own particular and **intimate** way.

Why not make my detective a Belgian? I thought. There were all types of refugees. How about a refugee police officer? A retired police officer. Not too young a one. What a mistake I made there. The result is that my **fictional** detective must really be well over a hundred by now.

Anyway, I settled on a Belgian detective. I allowed him slowly to grow into his part. He should have been an inspector, so that he would have a certain knowledge of crime. He would be **meticulous**, very tidy, I thought to myself, as I cleared away a good many untidy odds and ends in my own bedroom. A tidy little man. I could see him as a tidy little man, always arranging things, liking things in pairs, liking things square instead of round. And he should be very brainy — he should have little grey cells of the mind — that was a good phrase: I must remember that — yes, he would have little grey cells. He would have rather a grand name — one of those names that Sherlock Holmes and his family had. Who was it his brother had been? Mycroft Holmes.

How about calling my little man Hercules? He would be a small man — Hercules: a good name. His last name was more difficult. I don't know why I settled on the name Poirot; whether it just came into my head or whether I saw it in some newspaper or written on something — anyway it came. It went well not with Hercules but Hercule — Hercule Poirot. That was all right — settled, thank goodness.

Now I must get names for the others — but that was less important. Alfred Inglethorpe — that might do: it would go well with the black beard. I added some more characters. A husband and wife — attractive — **estranged** from each other. Now for all the **ramifications** — the false clues. Like all young writers, I was trying to put far too much plot into one book. I had too many false clues — so many things to unravel that it might make the whole thing not only more difficult to solve, but more difficult to read.

In leisure moments, bits of my detective story rattled about in my head. I had the beginning all settled, and the end arranged, but there were difficult gaps in between. I had Hercule Poirot involved in a natural and **plausible** way. But there had to be more reasons why other people were involved. It was still all in a tangle.

It made me absentminded at home. My mother was continually asking why I didn't answer questions or didn't answer them properly. I knitted Grannie's pattern wrong more than once; I forgot to do a lot of things that I was supposed to do; and I sent several letters to the wrong addresses. However, the time came when I felt I could at last begin to write. I told Mother what I was going to do. Mother had the usual complete faith that her daughters could do anything.

"Oh?" she said. "A detective story? That will be a nice change for you, won't it? You'd better start."

From Agatha Christie: An Autobiography, by Agatha Christie

★ Go back to the story. Underline any words or sentences that give you clues to the meanings of the **boldfaced** words. ★

85

USING CONTEXT

Meanings for the vocabulary words are given below. Go back to the story and read each sentence that contains a vocabulary word. If you still cannot tell the meaning, look for clues in the sentences that come before and after the one with the vocabulary word. Write each word beside its meaning.

refugees	fictional	plausible	parish
intimate	ramifications	journalist	emulate
estranged	meticulous		

1. _____ : made-up

2. _____ : imitate out of admiration

3. _____ : people who leave one place for another for reasons of safety; displaced persons

4. _____ : community or church district

5. _____ : separated; kept apart

6. _____ : very familiar; personal and private

7. _____ : consequences that are the result of something that has been said or done

8. _____ : appearing reasonable or true

9. _____ : very careful about details

10. _____ : person who writes or edits for a magazine or newspaper

CHALLENGE YOURSELF

Name two of your favorite characters from <u>fictional</u> stories.

_____   _____

Name two topics a <u>journalist</u> might write about.

_____   _____

Name two kinds of jobs that require <u>meticulous</u> work.

_____   _____

Name two personal qualities you would want to <u>emulate</u>.

_____   _____

ANALOGIES

An **analogy** shows the relationships between two pairs of words. Complete each of the following analogies by writing a word from the box on the line.

estranged	fictional	refugees
parish	journalist	meticulous

1. Hot is to cold as careless is to _____.

2. Awkward is to clumsy as separated is to _____.

3. Dancing is to ballerina as writing is to _____.

4. Joke is to comical as novel is to _____.

5. Country is to nation as community is to _____.

6. Wanderers are to nomads as exiles are to _____.

SYNONYMS

Synonyms are words that have the same or almost the same meaning. Write a word from the box that is a synonym of the underlined word in each sentence.

emulate	ramifications	fictional
intimate	plausible	

1. The young detective tried to copy the methods of his boss

   and _____ his style in handling cases.

2. The results of his investigation showed that there would be several

   _____ if the butler indeed committed the crime.

3. The detective realized that the butler was the only one involved with the personal details of the victim's life who

   had _____ information about the victim's family.

4. The butler gave some believable answers as to where he was when the crime was committed, and the detective had to admit they

   were _____.

5. In the end, however, the detective discovered the butler's story was

   made-up — every detail of it was _____.

GET WISE TO TESTS

Directions: Choose the word or words that best take the place of the boldfaced word.

This test will show you how well you understand the meaning of the words. Think about the meaning of the boldfaced word before you choose your answer.

1. The **journalist** enjoys her work. She writes about news events.
   Ⓐ pilot
   Ⓒ soloist
   Ⓑ artist
   Ⓓ reporter

2. We need to think about the **ramifications**. Problems could arise from one wrong move.
   Ⓕ wishes
   Ⓗ consequences
   Ⓖ leaders
   Ⓙ citation

3. That story is **fictional**. The events didn't really happen.
   Ⓐ truthful
   Ⓒ regional
   Ⓑ made-up
   Ⓓ ambitious

4. He is a **meticulous** worker. He pays close attention to details.
   Ⓕ miniature
   Ⓗ careless
   Ⓖ lazy
   Ⓙ careful

5. I record **intimate** thoughts in a diary. It is my private book.
   Ⓐ brilliant
   Ⓒ expensive
   Ⓑ personal
   Ⓓ invisible

6. They are **refugees**. They fled their country in search of safety.
   Ⓕ sailors
   Ⓗ syllables
   Ⓖ referees
   Ⓙ displaced persons

7. They do not belong to my **parish**. They live in an area far to the north.
   Ⓐ sports arena
   Ⓒ community
   Ⓑ private club
   Ⓓ family

8. The two friends are **estranged**. They no longer talk to one another.
   Ⓕ close
   Ⓗ separated
   Ⓖ interrupted
   Ⓙ established

9. Many try to **emulate** Robert Frost's poems. Few poets succeed, however, in writing as well.
   Ⓐ enjoy
   Ⓒ read
   Ⓑ imitate
   Ⓓ repair

10. That theory is **plausible**. It makes sense to almost every one.
    Ⓕ costly
    Ⓗ impossible
    Ⓖ hopeless
    Ⓙ believable

Review

1. The shipment was **intact**. Nothing was missing or damaged.
   Ⓐ horizontal
   Ⓒ whole
   Ⓑ broken
   Ⓓ recent

2. The wheels are in **alignment**. Now the car doesn't swerve.
   Ⓕ separate parts
   Ⓗ translation
   Ⓖ containers
   Ⓙ lined up accurately

Writing

Agatha Christie created a detective named Hercule Poirot. Other writers created famous detectives such as Charlie Chan and Sherlock Holmes. Pretend that you are a writer of detective stories. You need to make up a new detective who is thorough and clever — and always solves his or her cases! What will your detective look like? What name will you give to him or her?

On the lines below, write a description of your detective. Name him or her and include details that will help give a reader a clear picture of this person. Include things about his or her background and even some personal likes and dislikes. Use some vocabulary words in your writing.

_____

_____

_____

_____

_____

_____

_____

_____

_____

_____

_____

_____

_____

_____

_____

_____

_____

_____

Turn to "My Personal Word List" on page 132. Write some words from the story or other words that you would like to know more about. Use a dictionary to find the meanings.

★ Read the story below. Think about the meanings of the **boldfaced** words. ★

Triangle of Mystery

In a stretch of water between North and South America, the Atlantic Ocean and the Caribbean Sea meet. This region is referred to as "the Bermuda Triangle," after the nearby island of Bermuda. The mention of its name sends shivers down the spine of many a sailor and pilot.

Some people feel these fears are well-founded, for the Bermuda Triangle has had more than its share of unexplained catastrophes. They **acknowledge**, or admit, that this spot has over the years been the site of a series of strange — even **bizarre** — disappearances.

For example, in 1969, a pilot sent an odd communication to the control tower. She was circling over two islands, yet she could not see them. On one island, a group of hotel guests watched and waited expectantly for her to land. She disappeared shortly afterward and no trace of her or the aircraft was ever found. Everyone was **perplexed**, puzzled because the pilot had seen absolutely nothing below her, yet the people on the ground could clearly see her plane.

Other pilots have had their **perceptions** altered in the Bermuda Triangle and have seen strange things. Some have reported watching their instruments go wildly out of control on entering the Triangle. Even astronauts on board the Apollo space missions claimed seeing the area of the Triangle filled with huge foamy waves, waves that often signal great disturbances in nature.

These strange **circumstances**, or events, have led many people to **speculate** about what is causing these peculiar things to happen. Some writers have suggested the existence of a **mystical**, or supernatural, force that provides the energy to alter the real world.

Such explanations have led to disagreement. Most **oceanographic** scientists who study the world's seas believe that there is nothing unusual about the area. In their opinion, a disappearance is a **phenomenon**, or happening, that could occur anywhere in the world. That the Bermuda Triangle has had more than its share of disappearances they call an accident and purely **coincidental**. Yet belief in the Triangle's mystery persists. The fact remains that since 1854 more than fifty ships and airplanes have disappeared in or near the Bermuda Triangle. Most of them vanished without a trace.

★ Go back to the story. Underline the words or sentences that give you a clue to the meaning of each **boldfaced** word. ★

USING CONTEXT

Meanings for the vocabulary words are given below. Go back to the story and read each sentence that contains a vocabulary word. If you still cannot tell the meaning, look for clues in the sentences that come before and after the one with the vocabulary word. Write each word beside its meaning.

coincidental	bizarre	oceanographic	phenomenon
speculate	perplexed	circumstances	acknowledge
perceptions	mystical		

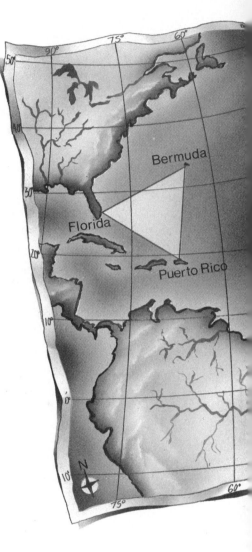

1. _____ : recognize a claim or truth about something; admit

2. _____ : puzzled; confused

3. _____ : relating to events happening at the same time apparently by chance, but seeming somehow planned

4. _____ : extremely strange

5. _____ : observations made through the use of the senses

6. _____ : existing conditions

7. _____ : think about carefully; guess

8. _____ : an event that can be observed

9. _____ : having to do with the study of the ocean or sea

10. _____ : mysterious; having some secret meaning

CHALLENGE YOURSELF

Name two things that might be studied by an <u>oceanographic</u> study group.

_____   _____

Name two things that have <u>perplexed</u> you.

_____   _____

Name two <u>circumstances</u> that would prevent you from going swimming.

_____   _____

WRITING SENTENCES

Write an original sentence with each of the words in the box.

acknowledge	mystical	perplexed	circumstances
coincidental	perceptions	oceanographic	

1. _____

2. _____

3. _____

4. _____

5. _____

6. _____

7. _____

CLOZE PARAGRAPH

Use the words in the box to complete the passage. Then reread the passage to be sure it makes sense.

circumstances	phenomenon	bizarre
speculated	perplexed	mystical

Have you ever witnessed an almost unexplainable

(1) _____? Has anyone ever told you about a strange experience that he or she has had?

Under unusual (2) _____, Mike once flew a sick child across the Bermuda Triangle in his airplane. Mike had

(3) _____ that, with clear skies, he could land in two

hours. Then, without warning, a (4) _____ thing happened. The plane began to shake and the needles on the instruments went out of control. Mike became frightened as he tried to keep the

plane steady. He was totally (5) _____. Was there

some (6) _____ force out there that would not allow him to complete his flight?!

Directions: Read the sentences. Look for the best word to use in the blank. Mark the answer space for your choice.

 Tip Some tests have letters inside the answer circles. Fill in the circle next to your answer, covering the letter, too.

1. The mask that Jan wore was very strange. It looked _____.
   - Ⓐ pleasant
   - Ⓒ coincidental
   - Ⓑ bizarre
   - Ⓓ silent

2. My neighbor and I ran into each other in another city. It was purely _____.
   - Ⓕ coincidental
   - Ⓗ oceanographic
   - Ⓖ important
   - Ⓙ critical

3. The heavy rain flooded the field, and the ground was muddy. Under these _____, the game could not be played.
   - Ⓐ athletes
   - Ⓒ opponents
   - Ⓑ circumstances
   - Ⓓ perceptions

4. That woman studies animals and plants in the sea. She is an _____ scientist.
   - Ⓕ easygoing
   - Ⓗ early
   - Ⓖ oceanographic
   - Ⓙ ancient

5. I felt as though I had been in that house before. It was a _____ experience.
   - Ⓐ mystical
   - Ⓒ fragile
   - Ⓑ oceanographic
   - Ⓓ carved

6. We admit that we broke the rules. We _____ our mistake.
   - Ⓕ speculate
   - Ⓗ reward
   - Ⓖ wonder
   - Ⓙ acknowledge

7. Millions of butterflies migrate south every year. It is an annual _____.
   - Ⓐ celebration
   - Ⓒ planet
   - Ⓑ perception
   - Ⓓ phenomenon

8. The child couldn't figure out how to do the puzzle. She was completely _____.
   - Ⓕ perplexed
   - Ⓗ retrieved
   - Ⓖ captured
   - Ⓙ expressed

9. In the desert, it is hard to judge distances. Your _____ may be thrown off.
   - Ⓐ phenomenon
   - Ⓒ perceptions
   - Ⓑ emotions
   - Ⓓ cactus

10. The experiment did not work. We can only _____ as to why it failed.
    - Ⓕ decide
    - Ⓗ acknowledge
    - Ⓖ revise
    - Ⓙ speculate

Review

1. She writes for a newspaper. She is a _____.
   - Ⓐ mechanic
   - Ⓒ coach
   - Ⓑ teacher
   - Ⓓ journalist

2. The jury thought that the witness was lying. His answers were not _____.
   - Ⓕ plausible
   - Ⓗ entertaining
   - Ⓖ cheerful
   - Ⓙ ridiculous

3. You can count on him for very careful work. He is _____.
   - Ⓐ sloppy
   - Ⓒ boring
   - Ⓑ meticulous
   - Ⓓ speedy

4. I have several heroes. I try to _____ their actions.
   - Ⓕ forget
   - Ⓗ criticize
   - Ⓖ emulate
   - Ⓙ ignore

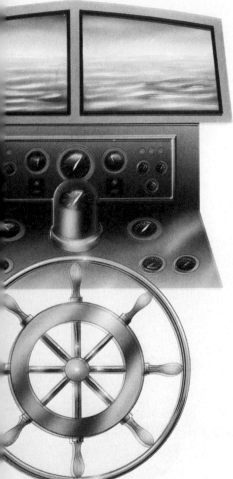

The reported wild reactions of instruments on ships and planes that have entered the Bermuda Triangle and the complete disappearance of many of those ships and planes have remained a great mystery. Oceanographic scientists believe that the disappearances within the Bermuda Triangle are just coincidental. Others believe that some unusual force of nature has played a part in those events. What do you think is the answer? Is it coincidence, or is there something happening beyond human understanding?

Write a paragraph expressing your views. Give reasons why you think as you do to help others understand your point of view. Use some vocabulary words in your writing.

Turn to "My Personal Word List" on page 132. Write some words from the story or other words that you would like to know more about. Use a dictionary to find the meanings.

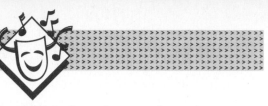

★ Read the story below. Think about the meanings of
the **boldfaced** words. ★

Statues That Wait

Easter Island is **situated** 2,400 miles west of Chile, in the South Pacific
Ocean. Geographically, there is nothing unusual about this island, yet it
is one of the most famous islands in the world. The Dutch were the first
to **colonize** Easter Island, bringing settlers from Europe in 1722. They
were also the first Westerners to see the remarkable sight that has
amazed people for over 250 years.

They found a series of fascinating sculptures — more than six
hundred of them — scattered over the island. Some of the sculptures
were carved in the shape of long, thin faces with no eyes. The faces
have long ears, jutting chins, and tiny legs. The sculptures'
adornments are only around their stomachs. The **artistry** used to
create the statues shows incredible skill. This is evident in the careful
carving and the precise placement of one stone on top of another. Some
of the statues had red stone cylinders balanced on their enormous heads
like hats, but all of these have long ago fallen off. Experts who have
studied the statues believe their creators carved them with hand picks
out of rock from an extinct volcano on the island.

Some of these **monumental** statues stand as tall as a three-story
house and weigh over fifty tons. Many people find it **incomprehensible**
that a primitive society could have moved such huge, bulky,
cumbersome stones and put them into place facing the ocean. They
cannot imagine these same people being sophisticated enough to carve
these artful figures and reject the entire idea.

Others have looked for an answer to why the mysterious statues
were built in the first place. Were they meant to represent something,
or have a **symbolic** purpose? One theory claims they were made to
commemorate, or honor the memory of, the builders' ancestors.
Another theory points to the fact that the statues look out to the ocean,
as though they were waiting for something. Perhaps the statues were
meant to form a **citadel**, or fort, to protect the islanders against a hostile
attack from the sea. A French writer who visited the island in 1870 put
it best when he wrote, "They have no eyes, only deep cavities under
their large, noble foreheads, yet they seem to be looking and
thinking . . . ."

★ Go back to the story. Underline the words or sentences that give you
a clue to the meaning of each **boldfaced** word. ★

CONTEXT CLUES

In each sentence a word or phrase is underlined. Choose a word from the box to replace that word or phrase. Write the word on the line.

situated	commemorate	citadel	colonize
cumbersome	incomprehensible	artistry	monumental
symbolic	adornments		

1. The statues of Easter Island surround the island like a

   protective <u>fort</u>. _____

2. The statues were <u>placed</u> so they would look out to the ocean.

   _____

3. The <u>skillful work of the artists</u> used to carve the faces is evident in

   all of the monuments. _____

4. Since the Dutch were the first to <u>settle</u> Easter Island, they were the

   first Westerners actually to see the statues._____

5. Visitors cannot imagine how the people of Easter Island were able
   to move the large stones that were <u>clumsy and difficult</u>

   <u>to manage</u>. _____

6. Today, the <u>massive</u> statues draw visitors from around the world.

   _____

7. Did these statues have a <u>representative</u> and special purpose for the

   ancient people of this place? _____

8. Many experts who study the statues find it <u>unbelievable</u> that a

   primitive society could build such objects._____

9. Perhaps the carving on the statues is there to <u>pay honor to</u> the
   builders' ancestors who first populated Easter Island.

   _____

10. The stone giants only have <u>decorations</u> around their stomachs.

    _____

MULTIPLE MEANINGS

The words in the box have more than one meaning. Look for clues in each sentence to tell which meaning is being used. Write the letter of the meaning next to the correct sentence.

monumental	citadel
a. huge or enormous in size	**a.** fort
b. very important	**b.** safe place

_____ 1. The pyramids of Egypt, like the statues of Easter Island, are <u>monumental</u> structures that rise high above the earth.

_____ 2. The discovery of the statues on Easter Island was <u>monumental</u> for those Westerners who study ancient cultures.

_____ 3. After the earthquake, the church became a <u>citadel</u> for those people forced out from their homes.

_____ 4. The <u>citadel</u> that housed the soldiers was made of heavy stones.

WORD GROUPS

As you read each pair of words, think about how they are alike. Write the word from the box that best completes each group.

citadel	incomprehensible	artistry	colonize
situated	adornments	symbolic	monumental
cumbersome	commemorate		

1. settle, establish,_____

2. craft, skill,_____

3. unbelievable, incredible,_____

4. bulky, awkward,_____

5. representative, meaningful,_____

6. honor, remember,_____

7. decorations, ornaments,_____

8. fort, refuge,_____

9. gigantic, massive,_____

10. placed, located,_____

FINE ARTS
THE UNEXPLAINABLE
LESSON 16

WORD MAP

Use the words in the box to complete the word map about the statues of
Easter Island. Add other words that you know to each category.

artistry	incomprehensible	citadel	monumental
cumbersome	adornments	symbolic	commemorate

What We See

1. _____
2. _____
3. _____
4. _____
5. _____

Purpose of the Statues

1. _____
2. _____
3. _____
4. _____
5. _____

EASTER ISLAND STATUES

Reactions to the Statues

1. _____
2. _____
3. _____
4. _____
5. _____

GET WISE TO TESTS

Directions: Read each sentence carefully. Then choose the best answer to complete each sentence. Mark the answer space for your choice.

Tip   Always read all the answer choices. Many choices may make sense. But only one choice has the same or almost the same meaning as the boldfaced word.

1. To **colonize** is to _____.
   - Ⓐ commemorate
   - Ⓑ destroy
   - Ⓒ settle
   - Ⓓ avoid

2. A **citadel** is a _____ used to protect people.
   - Ⓕ machine
   - Ⓖ potion
   - Ⓗ navy
   - Ⓙ fort

3. If something is **incomprehensible**, it is _____.
   - Ⓐ interesting
   - Ⓑ massive
   - Ⓒ upside-down
   - Ⓓ unbelievable

4. Things with **adornments** on them are _____.
   - Ⓕ ancient
   - Ⓖ decorated
   - Ⓗ awkward
   - Ⓙ full

5. If you know where something is **situated**, then you know where it is _____.
   - Ⓐ honored
   - Ⓑ located
   - Ⓒ decorated
   - Ⓓ managed

6. A **cumbersome** box is _____ to carry.
   - Ⓕ small
   - Ⓖ simple
   - Ⓗ awkward
   - Ⓙ symbolic

7. When you **commemorate** someone, you _____ that person.
   - Ⓐ meet
   - Ⓑ honor
   - Ⓒ trust
   - Ⓓ colonize

8. A building which is **monumental** is _____.
   - Ⓕ enormous
   - Ⓖ average
   - Ⓗ attractive
   - Ⓙ situated

9. A **symbolic** object is used to _____ something.
   - Ⓐ destroy
   - Ⓑ colonize
   - Ⓒ represent
   - Ⓓ reverse

10. The **artistry** of that design shows _____.
    - Ⓕ craziness
    - Ⓖ broken tools
    - Ⓗ skillfulwork
    - Ⓙ lazy work

Review

1. When you **acknowledge** a wrong, you _____ it.
   - Ⓐ commemorate
   - Ⓑ admit
   - Ⓒ deny
   - Ⓓ colonize

2. Something which is **bizarre** is _____.
   - Ⓕ strange
   - Ⓖ cumbersome
   - Ⓗ friendly
   - Ⓙ symbolic

3. A person who is **perplexed** is _____.
   - Ⓐ monumental
   - Ⓑ cumbersome
   - Ⓒ confused
   - Ⓓ situated

4. When you **speculate** about something, you _____ about it.
   - Ⓕ buy
   - Ⓖ guess
   - Ⓗ destroy
   - Ⓙ colonize

5. **Oceanographic** refers to the study of _____.
   - Ⓐ graphs
   - Ⓑ citadels
   - Ⓒ seas
   - Ⓓ artistry

6. A **mystical** experience is _____.
   - Ⓕ ordinary
   - Ⓖ expensive
   - Ⓗ cumbersome
   - Ⓙ mysterious

Writing

Think about the monuments of Stonehenge and Easter Island. How are they alike? How are they different?

Use the lines below to write a comparison of the monuments of Stonehenge and Easter Island. Include at least two similarities and two differences in your comparison. Use some vocabulary words in your writing.

Turn to "My Personal Word List" on page 132. Write some words from the story or other words that you would like to know more about. Use a dictionary to find the meanings.

★ To review the words in Lessons 13–16, turn to page 128. ★

URGENT: ENERGY

Our existence depends on many forms of energy. It can be provided by the wind, the sun, and fuel from the earth. It is even packed in dynamite and the food we digest.

In Lessons 17–20, you will read about types of energy, their sources, and their uses. Think about items in your kitchen that need energy to operate. Once the oven was the only appliance that used energy. Today there are microwave ovens, electric dishwashers, and so on. Where do they get their energy? Write your ideas on the lines below.

Things Requiring Energy	Sources of Energy

★ Read the story below. Think about the meanings of the **boldfaced** words. ★

Energy Crisis

Without energy, our world would come to a grinding halt. Cars wouldn't run, machines wouldn't work, and lights would go out, leaving us in darkness. This may sound like science fiction, but energy experts say in the not-too-distant future it could become fact.

Energy is a **commodity**, something that can be bought and sold. But it is a special commodity that is not made in the same way as other products you buy or sell. Energy sources — petroleum, coal, and natural gas — are fossil fuels that took millions of years to form. Once they are used, they cannot be quickly **replenished**, or restored, to keep up with an ever-increasing demand for energy.

Statistics show that our need for energy has increased over time. For example, in 1960 the United States consumed, or used, 45.12 quadrillion (a quadrillion is a million billion, or 1,000,000,000,000,000) British thermal units — Btu — of energy. By 1999, that figure had more than doubled, to 98 quadrillion Btu.

Conservationists who work to preserve our environment believe in the severity of a coming crisis and call for drastic action. These people say saving energy should not be a matter of **discretion**, left up to each person to decide. People's use of energy may need to be controlled or even rationed, they say.

But more important than this is the search for new energy sources to **compensate**, or make up for, shrinking supplies of fossil fuels. Scientists are studying ways of changing natural sources of energy into generated electricity. Rays from the sun, for example, can be changed into energy to heat homes and offices. Other possibilities are wind power and **geothermal** power. Geothermal power is generated when water comes into contact with hot underground rocks and steam is created. Engineers can also create geothermal power by shooting water onto hot rocks to form steam. The steam is then used to power machines that produce electricity. This kind of **conversion** of natural energy into other forms may one day be cheaper and more efficient than the energy sources we rely on today.

The **complexity** of our energy problems can seem overwhelming. There are many difficult problems to solve. But we can all take the first step by not being **wasteful** and by using energy resources wisely.

★ Go back to the story. Underline the words or sentences that give you a clue to the meaning of each **boldfaced** word. ★

Using Context

Meanings for the vocabulary words are given below. Go back to the story and read each sentence that contains a vocabulary word. If you still cannot tell the meaning, look for clues in the sentences that come before and after the one with the vocabulary word. Write each word beside its meaning.

statistics	wasteful	compensate	conversion
commodity	geothermal	complexity	conservationists
replenished	discretion		

1. _____: using or spending too much

2. _____: the quality of being difficult to understand or complicated

3. _____: filled again; furnished with a new supply

4. _____: numbers that give facts about people, places, and things

5. _____: anything bought and sold

6. _____: produced by heat within the earth

7. _____: make up for; to make an equal payment for

8. _____: freedom to act on one's own judgment; wise caution

9. _____: the act of changing; turning from one thing into another

10. _____: people who work to protect and save the natural resources of a country

CHALLENGE YOURSELF

Name two ways that people can be <u>wasteful</u>.

_____   _____

Name two things that <u>conservationists</u> might work to protect.

_____   _____

Along with <u>geothermal</u>, name two other natural sources of energy.

_____   _____

ANALOGIES

An **analogy** shows the relationship between two pairs of words. Complete each of the following analogies by writing a word from the box on the line.

| conservationists | geothermal | replenished |
| conversion | commodity | |

1. Heat is to solar as steam is to _____.

2. Purchased is to restocked as consumed is to _____.

3. Choice is to selection as change is to _____.

4. Shopper is to consumer as product is to _____.

5. Revolution is to revolutionaries as conservation is

   to _____.

WORD PAIRS

Words with similar parts may have related meanings. Study each word pair. Think about how the meanings of the words are alike. Check the meanings in the Dictionary. Then write a sentence for each word.

1. **discreet – discretion**

   _____

   _____

2. **compensate – compensation**

   _____

   _____

3. **wasteful – wastefulness**

   _____

   _____

4. **statistics – statistical**

   _____

   _____

5. **complex – complexity**

   _____

   _____

WORD GAME

The underlined letters in each sentence below can be used in one of the vocabulary words. Use the underlined letters and the context of the sentence to determine the correct vocabulary word. Write the word on the line.

commodity	statistics	wasteful	conservationist
conversion	replenished	compensate	discretion
geothermal	complexity		

1. He reached for his <u>pen</u> so that he could sign his employees' paychecks. _____

2. Concerned <u>as</u> she was about her grades, she still continued to misuse her time and her abilities. _____

3. When our neighbor returned all the tools he had borrowed, our once empty <u>shed</u> was again filled to capacity with equipment.

    _____

4. Don't try to <u>con</u> me into believing that this factory is not polluting the air, because I am one of those people who is working to

    protect the environment. _____

5. It was <u>her</u> theory that led them to try using steam as a source of energy. _____

6. Bill tried to persuade Greta to join his political party, but she was not willing to leave her own just <u>on</u> the advice of a friend.

    _____

7. The decision to have an operation on the <u>disc</u> in her back was left totally to the patient. _____

8. I can't find the <u>exit</u> because the design of this store is so involved that I keep running into more display counters.

    _____

9. With all these figures in front of me, I don't know <u>at</u> what point I'll find a solution. _____

10. A gold bracelet is not only beautiful, <u>it</u> is a good value in today's market. _____

GET WISE TO TESTS

Directions: Read the sentence or sentences. Look for the best word to use in the blank. Mark the answer space for your choice.

 Tip Before you choose an answer, try reading the sentence with each answer choice. This will help you choose an answer that makes sense.

1. She did not spend her money wisely. She was _____.
   Ⓐ meticulous   Ⓒ wasteful
   Ⓑ geothermal   Ⓓ mindful

2. No one could figure out a solution to the question. It was a problem of great _____.
   Ⓕ simplicity   Ⓗ astonishment
   Ⓖ legacy   Ⓙ complexity

3. Heat causes things to change. For example, it brings about the _____ of ice to water.
   Ⓐ complexity   Ⓒ loss
   Ⓑ conversion   Ⓓ freezing

4. The traveler was tired and hungry. But after a good meal, he felt _____.
   Ⓕ foolish   Ⓗ discretion
   Ⓖ replenished   Ⓙ complexity

5. Which states have the most rainfall? Look at the _____.
   Ⓐ conversion   Ⓒ thermometer
   Ⓑ sky   Ⓓ statistics

6. You are old enough to think for yourself. You must use your own _____.
   Ⓕ commodity   Ⓗ discretion
   Ⓖ anger   Ⓙ conservationists

7. We learned about underground springs. Some are created by _____ energy.
   Ⓐ geothermal   Ⓒ wasteful
   Ⓑ solar   Ⓓ wasted

8. The meeting was about ways to protect forests. Several _____ presented papers.
   Ⓕ commodities   Ⓗ audiences
   Ⓖ conservationists Ⓙ statistics

9. Thanks for your hard work. This extra pay will _____ you for your efforts.
   Ⓐ reduce   Ⓒ compensate
   Ⓑ irritate   Ⓓ bother

10. These gold coins are valuable. They are an important _____.
    Ⓕ complexity   Ⓗ commodity
    Ⓖ discretion   Ⓙ conversion

Review

1. The Rocky Mountains are east of California. They are _____ west of the Missouri River.
   Ⓐ surrounded   Ⓒ wandering
   Ⓑ situated   Ⓓ arrested

2. Many people from Sweden moved to Minnesota. They decided to _____ the area.
   Ⓕ converse   Ⓗ colonize
   Ⓖ activate   Ⓙ coordinate

3. The scouts joined in on the march. It was a _____ effort to protest the lack of housing.
   Ⓐ wasteful   Ⓒ symbolic
   Ⓑ roving   Ⓓ childish

4. The mail carrier has a heavy load in December. Many parcels are quite _____.
   Ⓕ acrobatic   Ⓗ conscious
   Ⓖ cumbersome   Ⓙ stubborn

Writing

Imagine that you have been asked to write an article about the energy crisis for your company newsletter. In the article, you are to outline ways people can be less wasteful of energy in their homes and at work.

Use the lines below to write this article. Be sure to review for your readers what the energy crisis is. Then suggest ways people can conserve energy. When you have completed your article, give it a title. Use some vocabulary words in your writing.

Turn to "My Personal Word List" on page 132. Write some words from the story or other words that you would like to know more about. Use a dictionary to find the meanings.

★ Read the story below. Think about the meanings of the **boldfaced** words. ★

Alfred Nobel: Dynamite and Prizes

Alfred Nobel's work with explosives made it possible to generate the energy necessary to build tunnels and dams through solid rock. His work also enabled him to establish the Nobel Prizes, which are given annually to professionals who have made outstanding contributions to peace, literature, science, or medicine.

One day in 1861, a group of Paris **financiers** gave impatient audience to a young Swedish inventor. He was a thin, sickly, nervous man, with penetrating blue eyes and plenty of assurance. He announced dramatically that he had an oil which would shake the globe.

Alfred Nobel calmly went on to explain his new explosive. After a while, they cut him off, ridiculing his claims. But when the Emperor Napoleon III heard about the violent oil, he didn't laugh. He used his influence, and Nobel went back to Stockholm with a draft for a hundred thousand francs. Within a year, he and his father were manufacturing **nitroglycerin** for commercial use. In a few years the world was startled by a new word—dynamite. And the foundation was laid for the Nobel fortune—the income from which is now distributed annually to scientists, writers, and workers for peace, for distinguished achievement in their fields.

To Alfred Nobel, there was nothing sinister about powerful explosives. He and his father and brothers had been working with them for years. Old Emmanuel, an architect turned inventor, could make anything from a field gun to a jack-in-the-box. He thought of using rubber for carriage tires and of using **porous** rubber cushions for carriage seats.

Emmanuel Nobel had become interested in the possibilities of nitroglycerin as an explosive. The **compound** had first been made in 1846 by Ascanio Sobrero, professor of chemistry at the University of Turin in Italy. He had discovered its explosive properties, but had decided that it was too dangerous.

Emmanuel and Alfred were less concerned about safety than was Sobrero. They mixed the oil with gunpowder, filled bombs with it, tossed the bombs into lakes and rivers, and watched columns of water

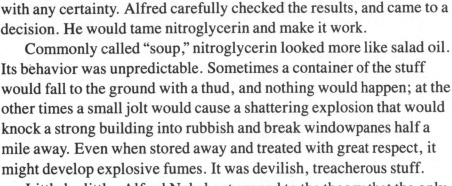

spurt up. This was risky business, for the reaction could not be plotted with any certainty. Alfred carefully checked the results, and came to a decision. He would tame nitroglycerin and make it work.

Commonly called "soup," nitroglycerin looked more like salad oil. Its behavior was unpredictable. Sometimes a container of the stuff would fall to the ground with a thud, and nothing would happen; at the other times a small jolt would cause a shattering explosion that would knock a strong building into rubbish and break windowpanes half a mile away. Even when stored away and treated with great respect, it might develop explosive fumes. It was devilish, treacherous stuff.

Little by little, Alfred Nobel got around to the theory that the only sure way of exploding this liquid was to confine it in a stout container and set it off with a sharp primary explosion. First he tried putting a glass tube of the soup into a metal container of gunpowder and setting off the powder with a fuse. Finally he **evolved** the blasting cap, a small copper cylinder filled with mercury fulminate and open at one end to permit the insertion of a fuse. In a nutshell: a match wouldn't explode nitroglycerin; it took force. So Nobel used an **intermediary** which would provide the force and could be set off with a match.

That invention is the basis of the whole nitroglycerin and dynamite industry. Nobel had found a way to explode the soup at will and with great effect. Today everyone who builds a dam, a canal, a subway, or a mountain road uses one of the descendants of "Nobel's Patent **Detonator**."

Even after Nobel had secured backing with the help of Napoleon, and he and his father had set up their first plant, Alfred's brothers were skeptical and tried to discourage him. "Give up inventing," Robert wrote from St. Petersburg. "You should turn your attention to more serious matters." That was in May, 1864. Four months later, Robert's **admonition** was given more weight by a ghastly tragedy.

Neither Emmanuel nor Alfred was in the shop that morning. The youngest son Emil, who was only twenty-one, was in charge. A mechanic and two other employees were there, and a passing workman had dropped in to see what was going on. There was an explosion, and everyone in the room was instantly killed.

Stockholm shook with terror at the news of the explosion, and wild rumors went around about the **eccentric** Nobels and the new monster which they had **unleashed**. But meanwhile, engineers and miners everywhere heard of the new timesaving, money-saving blasting oil. Orders and inquiries came in from all over the world.

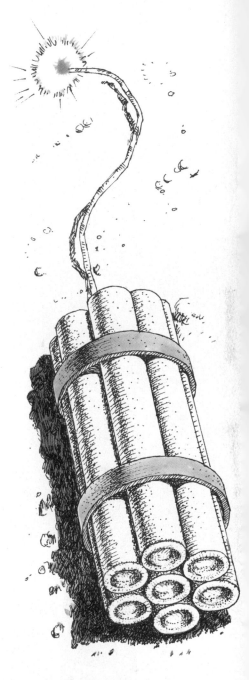

From Trail Blazers of Technology: The Story of Nine Inventors, by Harland Manchester

★ Go back to the story. Underline any words or sentences that give you clues to the meanings of the **boldfaced** words. ★

109

CONTEXT CLUES

In each sentence, a word or phrase is underlined. Choose a word from the box to replace that word or phrase. Write the word on the line.

intermediary	evolved	unleashed	eccentric
admonition	detonator	financiers	nitroglycerin
compound	porous		

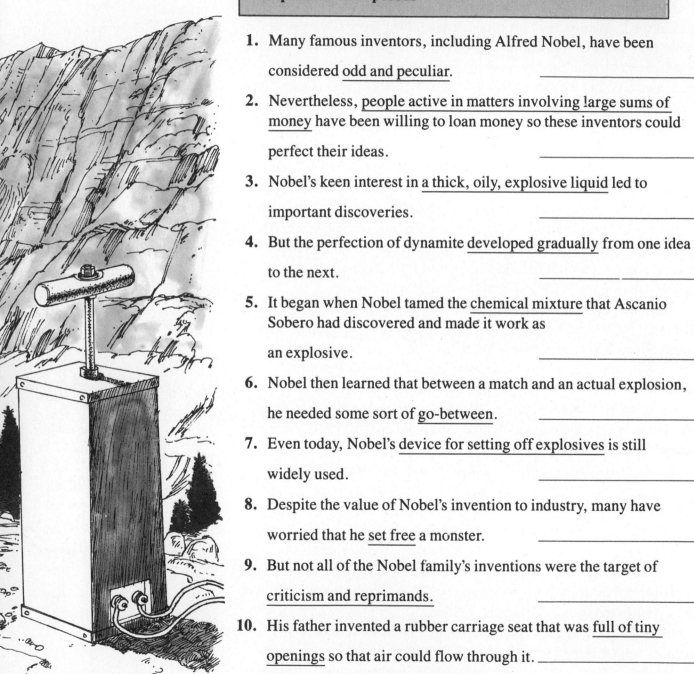

1. Many famous inventors, including Alfred Nobel, have been considered <u>odd and peculiar</u>. _____

2. Nevertheless, <u>people active in matters involving large sums of money</u> have been willing to loan money so these inventors could perfect their ideas. _____

3. Nobel's keen interest in <u>a thick, oily, explosive liquid</u> led to important discoveries. _____

4. But the perfection of dynamite <u>developed gradually</u> from one idea to the next. _____

5. It began when Nobel tamed the <u>chemical mixture</u> that Ascanio Sobero had discovered and made it work as an explosive. _____

6. Nobel then learned that between a match and an actual explosion, he needed some sort of <u>go-between</u>. _____

7. Even today, Nobel's <u>device for setting off explosives</u> is still widely used. _____

8. Despite the value of Nobel's invention to industry, many have worried that he <u>set free</u> a monster. _____

9. But not all of the Nobel family's inventions were the target of <u>criticism and reprimands</u>. _____

10. His father invented a rubber carriage seat that was <u>full of tiny openings</u> so that air could flow through it. _____

CHALLENGE YOURSELF

Name two things that are <u>porous</u>.

_____   _____

WORD GROUPS

As you read each pair of words, think about how they are alike. Write the word from the box that best completes each group.

financiers	porous	eccentric	evolved	nitroglycerin

1. perforated, punctured, _____

2. grew, developed, _____

3. bankers, investors, _____

4. gunpowder, TNT, _____

5. unusual, unique, _____

CONNOTATIONS

Some words are very close in meaning, yet there is a small difference between them. The words suggest slightly different things. This means that the words have different **connotations**. Read each sentence below. Choose a word from the box that has a slightly different connotation from the underlined word. Write the vocabulary word on the line.

intermediary	admonition	compound
eccentric	unleashed	detonator

1. The chemist created a new <u>mixture</u>, then shared the ingredients in

   the _____ with his students.

2. The pet shop employee accidentally <u>released</u> the dog, not realizing

   he had _____ a ferocious animal.

3. I received her <u>warning</u> silently, even though I felt

   the _____ was unfairly given.

4. I called the blasting cap an <u>exploder</u>, but my father, a construction

   engineer, corrected me, calling it a _____.

5. She was the <u>go-between</u>, carrying messages between the feuding

   friends, but she soon tired of playing _____.

6. They are a <u>curious</u> family whose unusual ways have earned them

   the reputation for being _____.

GET WISE TO TESTS

Directions: Choose the word or words that best take the place of the boldfaced word.

Tip Always read all the answer choices. Many choices may make sense, but only one answer choice has the same or almost the same meaning as the boldfaced word.

1. A new theory **evolved**. It was the result of years of work.
   - Ⓐ dissolved
   - Ⓑ developed
   - Ⓒ revolved
   - Ⓓ erupted

2. Be careful with the **compound**. It can be explosive.
   - Ⓕ contraction
   - Ⓖ intermediary
   - Ⓗ pore
   - Ⓙ mixture

3. This sounds like another **admonition**. He thinks I'll do wrong.
   - Ⓐ advertisement
   - Ⓑ warning
   - Ⓒ promise
   - Ⓓ gift

4. Call an **intermediary**. We can't seem to resolve this problem between the two of us.
   - Ⓕ go-between
   - Ⓖ police
   - Ⓗ eccentric
   - Ⓙ leader

5. That is a **detonator**. It must be used with great caution.
   - Ⓐ toner
   - Ⓑ lotion
   - Ⓒ exploding device
   - Ⓓ opening device

6. They are **financiers**. They are knowledgeable about money management.
   - Ⓕ detonators
   - Ⓖ investors
   - Ⓗ writers
   - Ⓙ shoppers

7. Our skin is **porous**. It can breathe.
   - Ⓐ full of tiny holes
   - Ⓑ porcelain
   - Ⓒ full of tiny hairs
   - Ⓓ important

8. She is **eccentric**. No one I know behaves that way.
   - Ⓕ centered
   - Ⓖ ecstatic
   - Ⓗ unusual
   - Ⓙ exceptional

9. Keep away from **nitroglycerin**. It can blow up this room.
   - Ⓐ liquid detergent
   - Ⓑ liquid explosive
   - Ⓒ solid detergent
   - Ⓓ solid explosive

10. Some thought Nobel **unleashed** a monster. Explosives are dangerous, but also useful.
    - Ⓕ evolved
    - Ⓖ destroyed
    - Ⓗ warned
    - Ⓙ released

Review

1. Here are the **statistics**. They show how many students play tennis.
   - Ⓐ plans
   - Ⓑ numbers
   - Ⓒ rackets
   - Ⓓ letters

2. Use your **discretion**. I know you will make a wise decision.
   - Ⓕ creativity
   - Ⓖ commodities
   - Ⓗ judgment
   - Ⓙ imagination

Writing

The Nobel family earned a vast fortune from the sale of dynamite. Before he died, Alfred Nobel requested that the money be used to award yearly prizes to people who make great achievements in the sciences, economics, and literature. Nobel also wanted to honor people who work for peace. So each year the Nobel Peace Prize is given to an individual or organization that has done the most to promote world peace.

Imagine you are in charge of awarding the Nobel Peace Prize this year. Think about who you think deserves the award. Describe that person or group and their work in a paragraph. Use some vocabulary words in your writing.

_____

_____

_____

_____

_____

_____

_____

_____

_____

_____

_____

_____

_____

Turn to "My Personal Word List" on page 132. Write some words from the story or other words that you would like to know more about. Use a dictionary to find the meanings.

★ Read the story below. Think about the meanings of the **boldfaced** words. ★

Flying with the Sun

Inventor Paul MacCready was a man with a mission – to get people to solve their present-day problems by looking back to the past or forward to the future. One of MacCready's more famous projects did both. His plane, the *Solar Challenger,* looked like something the Wright brothers might have built, but it was designed to operate on the energy of the sun. It was not the first plane to attempt to **harness** solar energy and put it to work, but it was the first to do so without storing the energy in batteries before taking off.

At only 217 pounds, the *Solar Challenger* definitely qualified as **lightweight**. It was a **monoplane** – an aircraft with a single set of wings. It got its power from more than 16,000 solar cells spread over the wings and the rear section of the plane. These cells collected energy from the sun and converted it to electricity, which was then **conducted** through wires to the engine.

The maiden flight of the *Solar Challenger* in 1981 had its ups and downs. On an airport runway in Paris, France, the pilot repeatedly attempted to get the plane off the ground without success. Finally, the aircraft slowly rose into the air. When he saw the **altimeter** reading of 250 feet, the pilot was very relieved. The *Solar Challenger* eventually reached an altitude of 11,000 feet. As the pilot **accelerated** to a speed of forty-seven miles per hour, the plane headed across the English Channel. Powered only by the sun and its own **kinetic** energy – the energy an object has because it is already in motion – the *Solar Challenger* completed its voyage. It landed in Dover, England, five hours and twenty-three minutes after takeoff.

Admittedly, a plane that can fly only when the sun is shining is not very practical. The flight of the *Solar Challenger* demonstrated that solar energy is an **accessible** energy source that can be obtained easily. MacCready believed that inventions like his could be **modified**, or changed, for more practical uses. He continued to explore ways to use the sun's power to drive **mechanized**, or machine-run, vehicles, inventing *Sunraycer,* a solar car, and *Gossamer Penguin,* another solar-powered plane. Today MacCready continues to develop new environmentally sound methods of transporting peoples.

★ Go back to the story. Underline the words or sentences that give you a clue to the meaning of each **boldfaced** word. ★

CONTEXT CLUES

Read each sentence. Look for clues to help you complete each sentence with a word from the box. Write the word on the line.

monoplane	accessible	mechanized	modified
harness	accelerated	conducted	lightweight
kinetic	altimeter		

1. In today's _____ society, most work is done by machines.

2. But as more power is needed, people have _____, or altered, their ideas about possible energy sources.

3. Paul MacCready had an idea for an airplane that used the sun's energy and its own _____ energy, the energy of motion, for its power.

4. MacCready had been working slowly on the plane for several years, but when the energy shortage began in the 1970s, he _____ his efforts.

5. Called the *Solar Challenger*, this _____ had only one set of wings.

6. Unlike planes built of heavy materials, the *Solar Challenger* was made of a _____ plastic and weighed only 217 pounds.

7. Special energy cells collected the solar energy and converted it to electricity, which was _____ to the engine.

8. The test pilot flew the plane at a height of 11,000 feet, as measured by the _____, the altitude gauge in the plane.

9. The successful flight of the *Solar Challenger* proved that people can _____, or control and use, the sun's energy.

10. But solar energy is _____ only when the sun shines!

CHALLENGE YOURSELF

Name two other natural sources of energy that people have been able to harness.

_____   _____

A Solar-Powered Vehicle

accelerated
altimeter
monoplane
accessible
kinetic

MULTIPLE MEANINGS

The words in the box have more than one meaning. Look for clues in each sentence to tell which meaning is being used. Write the letter of the meaning next to the correct sentence.

lightweight **a.** not heavy **b.** not important	**conducted** **a.** transmitted **b.** led a musical group
harness **a.** straps used to control an animal **b.** to control and put to work	**modified** **a.** changed slightly **b.** made less extreme or severe

1. A windmill can be used to harness the wind.

2. In view of all their troubles, my problems are lightweight.

3. The copper frying pan conducted the heat evenly.

4. We modified our decision and said Lil would be confined to the house for only a week instead of a whole month.

5. The orchestra was conducted by a famous musician.

6. Although this is a lightweight aluminum, it is very strong.

7. We modified our plans so we would be home a day earlier.

8. The mule was fastened to the plow with a harness.

CLOZE PARAGRAPH

Use the words in the box to complete the passage. Then reread the passage to be sure it makes sense.

My wife gave me a glider trip for Christmas. I never thought that such an experience would be (1) _____ to me. I was elated when we approached the airport and I caught my first glimpse of the (2) _____ tied down in the hangar.

My moment had finally arrived, and I could feel the breeze race over my face as we (3) _____ after takeoff. After we evened off, the navigator checked the (4) _____ and appeared content with our altitude. Powered only by the wind and its own (5) _____ energy, our glider soared with the eagles for over an hour.

Directions: Read each sentence carefully. Then choose the best answer to complete each sentence. Mark the space for the answer you have chosen.

Tip This test will show how well you understand the meaning of the words. Think about the meaning of the boldfaced word before you choose your answer.

1. An **altimeter** measures an object's _____.
   - Ⓐ altitude
   - Ⓒ width
   - Ⓑ length
   - Ⓓ weight

2. Something which is **accessible** is _____.
   - Ⓕ worthless
   - Ⓗ expensive
   - Ⓖ obtainable
   - Ⓙ breakable

3. A **monoplane** has _____.
   - Ⓐ one wheel
   - Ⓒ one set of wings
   - Ⓑ one motion
   - Ⓓ one window

4. **Kinetic** refers to _____.
   - Ⓕ business
   - Ⓗ movement
   - Ⓖ kindness
   - Ⓙ speech

5. By building a dam, you can **harness** the _____ of water.
   - Ⓐ taste
   - Ⓒ freshness
   - Ⓑ power
   - Ⓓ beauty

6. Work that is **mechanized** is done by _____.
   - Ⓕ males
   - Ⓗ hand
   - Ⓖ females
   - Ⓙ machines

7. When a car is **accelerated**, it is _____.
   - Ⓐ sped up
   - Ⓒ turned
   - Ⓑ slowed down
   - Ⓓ suddenly stopped

8. **Conducted** electricity is _____.
   - Ⓕ shocking
   - Ⓗ full
   - Ⓖ ancient
   - Ⓙ transmitted

9. A **modified** plan is _____.
   - Ⓐ approved
   - Ⓒ shipped
   - Ⓑ rejected
   - Ⓓ changed

10. _____ is a **lightweight** material used to make warm-weather clothing.
    - Ⓕ Wool
    - Ⓗ Cotton
    - Ⓖ Fur
    - Ⓙ Velvet

Review

1. **Financiers** deal with _____.
   - Ⓐ exports
   - Ⓒ fitness
   - Ⓑ money
   - Ⓓ decorations

2. An **intermediary** is one who _____ two people.
   - Ⓕ goes between
   - Ⓗ likes
   - Ⓖ fights
   - Ⓙ knows

3. **Nitroglycerin** is an _____.
   - Ⓐ explosive idea
   - Ⓒ oily rock
   - Ⓑ awful attitude
   - Ⓓ explosive liquid

4. If you have been given an **admonition**, you have been _____.
   - Ⓕ praised
   - Ⓗ dismissed
   - Ⓖ warned
   - Ⓙ rewarded

5. A **detonator** is used to _____.
   - Ⓐ test sounds
   - Ⓒ stop bombs
   - Ⓑ make maps
   - Ⓓ set off explosives

6. An **unleashed** dog is _____.
   - Ⓕ freed
   - Ⓗ groomed
   - Ⓖ captured
   - Ⓙ purchased

Even before the successful flight of the *Solar Challenger,* Paul MacCready had been experimenting with airplanes that were powered by alternative sources of energy. In 1977, he introduced a bicycle-like plane. It was powered by human energy and could be kept in the air by pedaling it.

Imagine that you are Paul MacCready's assistant. On the lines below, send a memo to Dr. MacCready. In your memo, suggest an idea for an invention that he might work on that would use an unusual energy source. Be sure to explain how the invention would be operated. Use your imagination—the energy source doesn't have to be a familiar one. Use some vocabulary words in your writing.

TO: Dr. Paul MacCready

FROM: _____

DATE: _____

_____

_____

_____

_____

_____

_____

_____

_____

_____

_____

_____

_____

_____

_____

Turn to "My Personal Word List" on page 132. Write some words from the story or other words that you would like to know more about. Use a dictionary to find the meanings.

★ Read the story below. Think about the meanings of the **boldfaced** words. ★

Food into Energy

The human body is a kind of machine, and like any machine, it needs energy to do its work. The energy comes from the food you **consume**. After you chew and swallow food, it is broken down into small pieces and converted into the energy your body needs. This process is called **digestion**. The digestive system uses certain nourishing parts of food – called **nutrients** – for energy.

Most of the work of digesting food takes place in the stomach, where the food is mixed with various body fluids. These digestive fluids, or **enzymes**, break down the food into its basic chemicals, the same chemicals your body requires to stay physically fit. Some enzymes work only on **proteins**, nutrients made of nitrogen and found in meat, milk, eggs, and other foods. Other enzymes work only on **carbohydrates**, the sugars and starches found in such foods as candy, rice, and bread.

Digestion is completed in the small intestine, and the digested food enters your bloodstream through a process called **absorption**. After your body takes in the food, the blood carries it to muscles, bones, and other parts of the body. Your body uses the chemicals for energy to shoot a basketball or read this page. They also provide energy for your growth and for the repairing of cells. The amount of energy that the body needs varies from one individual to another. Children generally need more energy than adults and larger people need more than smaller people.

The energy in food is measured in **calories**. A calorie is a unit used to measure the amount of energy supplied by foods. Most teenagers need about three thousand calories a day to stay healthy and active. When people do not eat sufficent quantities of nourishing foods, a **deficiency** of energy results. When this shortage becomes serious, the body suffers from **malnutrition**. Malnutrition can result from too little food or too much of the wrong kinds of food.

To stay healthy, a person should eat a balanced diet. That means eating foods from each of the four food groups. It's not hard to do, and the reward is a body that is in top shape and full of energy!

★ Go back to the story. Underline the words or sentences that give you a clue to the meaning of each **boldfaced** word. ★

USING CONTEXT

Meanings for the vocabulary words are given below. Go back to the story and read each sentence that contains a vocabulary word. If you still cannot tell the meaning, look for clues in the sentences that come before and after the one with the vocabulary word. Write each word beside its meaning.

nutrients	proteins	absorption	malnutrition
consume	enzymes	deficiency	carbohydrates
calories	digestion		

1. _____: shortage; a lack of something required

2. _____: to eat or drink; to use up

3. _____: nutritious substances that are necessary for proper body functioning

4. _____: the process by which the body breaks down food in the stomach to use as energy

5. _____: chemical compounds such as starches and sugars

6. _____: units used to measure the amount of energy supplied by various foods

7. _____: a condition in which the body suffers from a lack of nutritious substances

8. _____: chemical substances that help break down foods in the body

9. _____: the process by which food enters the bloodstream after it has been broken down

10. _____: chemical compounds that contain nitrogen and are found in meat, milk, and fish

CHALLENGE YOURSELF

Name two foods that are high in carbohydrates.

_____   _____

REWRITING SENTENCES

Rewrite each sentence using one of the vocabulary words from the box.

malnutrition	enzymes	carbohydrates	consume

1. He follows a diet low in sugars and starches.

   _____

2. Chemical substances help your body digest food.

   _____

3. To lose weight, you must exercise more and eat less food.

   _____

4. The doctor found that the child suffered from a lack of nourishment.

   _____

CLOZE PARAGRAPH

Use the words in the box to complete the passage. Then reread the passage to be sure it makes sense.

carbohydrates	nutrients	protein	absorption
digestion	consume	calories	deficiency

Are you eating the right foods, ones that provide all the

(1) _____ your body needs? Doctors recommend

that teenagers (2) _____ about 3,000

(3) _____ a day. That may sound like you can eat a
lot, but foods like potato chips and doughnuts will quickly add up!

To avoid any kind of vitamin or mineral (4) _____,
or shortage, you must eat a balanced diet. This means eating plenty of
fruits and vegetables, plus foods like pasta and rice, which are high in

(5) _____. You should also eat foods like chicken and

fish, which are high in (6) _____. An added bonus
for eating the right kinds of foods is that they do not cause problems in

the stomach when it is time for (7) _____ to begin.

Once they are broken down, (8) _____ of the
nutrients into the bloodstream takes place smoothly. So eat right!

121

TANGLED-UP WORDS

In the following passage, the underlined words do not make sense. But each sounds similar to a word in the box. Study the context in which the underlined words appear. For each word, find the word in the box that should be used in its place. Write the correct word on the numbered line.

nutrients	proteins	absorption	deficiency
consume	calories	malnutrition	carbohydrates
enzymes	digestion		

In many ways, the human body is like a machine. You give it energy in the form of food and it runs. But you can't feed it just any foods. It needs foods that contain the (1) <u>nuclears</u> that keep it running in top form.

There are many vitamins and minerals your body needs that you must make sure are contained in the foods you eat. Your body also needs certain (2) <u>proceeds</u> found in meat, milk, and fish. Your body depends on the (3) <u>carpenters</u> you (4) <u>assume</u> for high energy. Haven't you noticed that when you eat foods that contain sugar or starch, such as candy or potatoes, that you have more get-up-and-go? But beware! Those same foods are also high in (5) <u>canneries</u>. To stay slim, you must eat them in moderation.

What happens to your body when you don't eat the right foods? The machine won't work right. One sign of problems may occur when (6) <u>suggestion</u> is taking place in your stomach. Very spicy or rich foods may be difficult for the (7) <u>engines</u> to break down and may make you feel uncomfortable. But even more serious problems will develop if you are not taking in enough vitamins and minerals. Then you may develop a (8) <u>democracy</u>.

The most serious condition occurs when your body is deprived of healthful foods for a long time. Then it can develop (9) <u>malfunction</u>. This means that when the process of (10) <u>abbreviation</u> takes place, very few healthful substances are absorbed into the bloodstream.

However, there is no need for these serious problems to occur. All your body needs to hum along like a well-tuned machine is a healthful diet. Give your body what it needs. You deserve it!

1. _____

2. _____

3. _____

4. _____

5. _____

6. _____

7. _____

8. _____

9. _____

10. _____

Directions: Read each sentence. Pick the word that best completes the sentence. Mark the answer space for that word.

 Tip If you are not sure which word completes the sentence, do the best you can. Try to choose the answer that makes the most sense.

1. Food enters the bloodstream through a process called _____.
   - Ⓐ consume
   - Ⓑ swift
   - Ⓒ important
   - Ⓓ absorption

2. The very thin child was suffering from _____.
   - Ⓕ malnutrition
   - Ⓖ sickly
   - Ⓗ intruder
   - Ⓙ absorption

3. There are about three hundred _____ in this dessert.
   - Ⓐ delicious
   - Ⓑ chewing
   - Ⓒ calories
   - Ⓓ digestion

4. We must eat more foods rich in vitamins to avoid a _____ in our diets.
   - Ⓕ devoured
   - Ⓖ deficiency
   - Ⓗ ate
   - Ⓙ calorie

5. Food is broken down in the body by _____.
   - Ⓐ fire
   - Ⓑ swallowed
   - Ⓒ enzymes
   - Ⓓ consume

6. Potatoes, breads, and cereals are _____.
   - Ⓕ serves
   - Ⓖ eating
   - Ⓗ calories
   - Ⓙ carbohydrates

7. The label on the jar listed the _____ it contained.
   - Ⓐ digestion
   - Ⓑ nutrients
   - Ⓒ tempting
   - Ⓓ resume

8. This portion is so large, I can't _____ all of it.
   - Ⓕ nutrients
   - Ⓖ finishing
   - Ⓗ consume
   - Ⓙ calories

9. Drinking water aids in the _____ of food.
   - Ⓐ digestion
   - Ⓑ nutrients
   - Ⓒ sipped
   - Ⓓ slippery

10. For the growth and repair of the body, _____ are important.
   - Ⓕ consume
   - Ⓖ proteins
   - Ⓗ restful
   - Ⓙ exercised

Review

1. I am wearing a _____ jacket because it is a warm day.
   - Ⓐ warmth
   - Ⓑ lightweight
   - Ⓒ furry
   - Ⓓ heavyweight

2. Wires _____ the current to the store.
   - Ⓕ welcomed
   - Ⓖ singing
   - Ⓗ conducted
   - Ⓙ mention

3. The _____ has one pair of wings.
   - Ⓐ motorcycle
   - Ⓑ activate
   - Ⓒ monoplane
   - Ⓓ flying

4. The modern factory is _____.
   - Ⓕ mechanized
   - Ⓖ destruct
   - Ⓗ falls
   - Ⓙ hours

5. The racer _____ her speed in order to win.
   - Ⓐ losing
   - Ⓑ accelerated
   - Ⓒ rush
   - Ⓓ slowly

Writing

Imagine that you are going to be the host of a party. You want to present your guests with healthful, tasty foods. What foods would you serve to your friends?

Write a paragraph in which you describe the menu you would plan for your party. For each food on the menu, remember to include your reason for this healthful choice. Use some vocabulary words in your writing.

_____

_____

_____

Turn to "My Personal Word List" on page 132. Write some words from the story or other words that you would like to know more about. Use a dictionary to find the meanings.

_____

_____

_____

_____

_____

_____

★ To review the words in Lessons 17–20, turn to page 129. ★

REVIEW

Read each question. Think about the meaning of the underlined word. Then use yes or no to answer the question. Use the Dictionary if you need help.

1. If you wanted to be a movie star, would charisma be a good thing to have? _____

2. If you need to see something minuscule, would a microscope help? _____

3. If you are trying to find the density of an object, are you trying to measure its height? _____

4. Are your grandparents your descendants? _____

5. If you want someone to laugh at your jokes, should you find someone who is impervious to your humor? _____

6. Can you pour liquid into a vial? _____

7. If your puppy is sick, should you take it to a pediatrician? _____

8. If you practice a speech over and over, have you immersed it? _____

9. When scientists demonstrated that the earth is round, did they prove their point? _____

10. If you want to win an Olympic gold medal in swimming, would being paralytic come in handy? _____

11. Would a surgical team perform a heart operation? _____

12. Would bedrock probably be comfortable to sleep on? _____

13. If you have multifarious talents, should you see a doctor? _____

14. Would an optimistic person look on the bright side of things? _____

15. If you are adjacent to your desk, are you sitting at it?

_____

125

REVIEW

Read each clue. Then write the word from the box that fits the clue. Use the Dictionary if you need help.

outmoded	transistors	simplifying	initiative
envision	contemporary	misbehaving	primarily
skeptical	dilemma	educator	glitch

1. If you are typing on your computer and the screen goes blank, your computer may be experiencing this. _____

2. If your parents replaced the living room furniture with new, modern pieces, the look of the room might be described as this.

   _____

3. If you must choose between the lesser of two evils, this is what you face. _____

4. If your best friend told you he was actually Batman, you would probably feel this way. _____

5. A student who is talking without permission is doing this.

   _____

6. Traveling by horse and buggy could be described as this.

   _____

7. If you mow yards all summer in order to save money for a car, you are showing this. _____

8. When you picture yourself skiing down a mountain, you do this.

   _____

9. If you plan to pursue a career as a teacher, this is what you want to be. _____

10. If you are using a computer program to check your spelling, you are doing this to the job of proofreading. _____

11. You could find these inside of your television set.

    _____

12. You can often use this word instead of <u>mainly</u>.

    _____

Read each question. Think about the meaning of the underlined word. Then use <u>yes</u> or <u>no</u> to answer the question. Use the Dictionary if you need help.

1. Could you call a forest where no one has been <u>unspoiled</u>? _____

2. If you need to be sure that an old painting was done by a famous artist, do you need someone to <u>authenticate</u> it? _____

3. Would most people say that a trash dump has <u>magnificence</u>? _____

4. If you <u>equalized</u> the number of pennies you held in each hand, would one hand have the same number as the other? _____

5. Could you buy <u>motivation</u> at a hardware store? _____

6. If you want to improve your spelling, should you study <u>speleology</u>? _____

7. Is it possible to <u>visualize</u> how you want to spend the summer? _____

8. If you want to find a cave, should you look for a <u>cavity</u>? _____

9. Would it be easy to write about something that is <u>indescribable</u>? _____

10. Is a tropical beach normally <u>dank</u>? _____

11. If a fact is <u>indelibly</u> imprinted on your mind, will you remember it the next day? _____

12. If you are having trouble with your car, will changing your <u>attire</u> help? _____

13. If your interest in flying has been <u>whetted</u>, would you then want to learn more about it? _____

14. Could an <u>alcove</u> be a good place to hide from a giant? _____

15. Would a <u>maw</u> be useful for playing baseball? _____

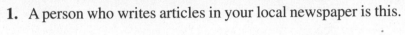

Read each clue. Then write the word from the box that fits the clue. Use the Dictionary if you need help.

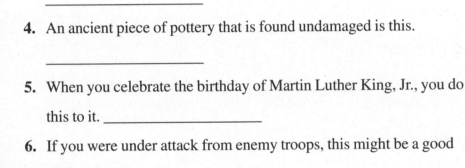

coincidental	acknowledge	intact	colonize
emulate	symmetry	journalist	sightseers
estranged	commemorate	citadel	perplexed

1. A person who writes articles in your local newspaper is this.
   _____

2. When you act just like your older brother or sister, you do this.
   _____

3. These people like to take vacations to new places.
   _____

4. An ancient piece of pottery that is found undamaged is this.
   _____

5. When you celebrate the birthday of Martin Luther King, Jr., you do this to it. _____

6. If you were under attack from enemy troops, this might be a good place to go. _____

7. Two people who are no longer friends could be described as this.
   _____

8. When you are working on a difficult math problem, you might feel this way. _____

9. If you are thinking of a friend and she phones you at that moment, the situation could be described as this. _____

10. The first people to move into a new region do this.
    _____

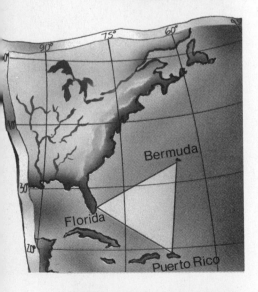

11. Because each half of a butterfly is the same lengthwise, we say it has this. _____

12. If you tell your boss you've done something wrong, you do this to your mistake. _____

REVIEW

Read each clue. Then write the word from the box that fits the clue. Use the Dictionary if you need help.

admonition	consume	intermediary	accessible
enzymes	accelerated	malnutrition	wasteful
harness	eccentric	replenished	conservationists

1. If you walked from room to room on your hands, you might be called this. _____

2. This is the result of not eating properly for a long time.
   _____

3. A person who drove a car faster and faster did this.
   _____

4. If you help two friends settle a disagreement, you could be called this. _____

5. If you went to the store and bought groceries for your empty refrigerator, you did this to your food supply.
   _____

6. If you eat a pizza, you do this to it. _____

7. People who plant trees and recycle could be called this.
   _____

8. A windmill must do this to the wind to create energy.
   _____

9. This is what you might give your class if they misbehave.
   _____

10. If you need information that is easy to find, you need this kind of data. _____

11. Without these, digestion would be impossible.
    _____

12. Someone who throws away perfectly good food could be described with this word. _____

REVIEW AND WRITE

Think about some of the men and women you have read about in *Vocabulary Connections*.

Antoni van Leeuwenhoek

Rear Admiral Grace Hopper

Jon Lindbergh

Agatha Christie

Alfred Nobel

Dr. Benjamin Carson

Paul MacCready

Imagine if they were able to meet each other. What would they discuss? What might Rear Admiral Grace Murray say about her work with computers to Agatha Christie? What might Antoni van Leeuwenhoek and Jon Lindbergh tell one another about their discoveries? Choose two of the people you find to be the most interesting. Then write an imaginary conversation between them. Use some vocabulary words you have learned.

_____

_____

_____

_____

_____

_____

_____

_____

MY PERSONAL WORD LIST

This is your word list. Here you can write words from the stories. You can also write other words that you would like to know more about. Use a dictionary to find the meaning of each word. Then write the meaning next to the word.

UNIT 1
GREAT CONNECTIONS

_____

_____

_____

_____

_____

_____

_____

_____

UNIT 2
THE COMPUTER AGE

_____

_____

_____

_____

_____

_____

_____

_____

MY PERSONAL WORD LIST

UNIT 3
CAVES AND CAVERNS

_____

_____

_____

_____

_____

_____

_____

_____

UNIT 4
THE UNEXPLAINABLE

_____

_____

_____

_____

_____

_____

_____

_____

UNIT 5
URGENT: ENERGY

_____

_____

_____

_____

_____

_____

_____

_____

MY PERSONAL WORD LIST

DICTIONARY

ENTRY

Each word in a dictionary is called an **entry word**. Study the parts of an entry in the sample shown below. Think about how each part will help you when you read and write.

① **Entry Word** An entry word is boldfaced. A dot is used to divide the word into syllables.

② **Pronunciation** This special spelling shows you how to say the word. Look at the pronunciation key below. It tells you the symbols that stand for sounds.

③ **Part of Speech** The abbreviation tells you the part of speech. In this entry *v.* stands for verb.

④ **Words with Spelling Changes** When the spelling of a word changes after *-ed* or *-ing* is added, the spelling is shown in an entry.

⑤ **Definition** A definition is given for each entry word. The definition tells what the word means.

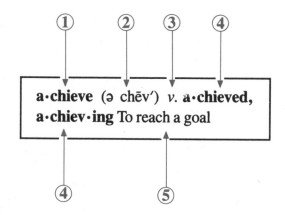

PRONUNCIATION KEY

A **pronunciation key** is a helpful tool. It shows you the symbols, or special signs, for the sounds in English. Next to each symbol is a sample word for that sound. Use the key to help you with the pronunciation given after each entry word.

a	at, bad		d	dear, soda, bad
ā	ape, pain, day, break		f	five, defend, leaf, off, cough, elephant
ä	father, car, heart		g	game, ago, fog, egg
âr	care, pair, bear, their, where		h	hat, ahead
e	end, pet, said, heaven, friend		hw	white, whether, which
ē	equal, me, feet, team, piece, key		j	joke, enjoy, gem, page, edge
i	it, big, English, hymn		k	kite, bakery, seek, tack, cat
ī	ice, fine, lie, my		l	lid, sailor, feel, ball, allow
îr	ear, deer, here, pierce		m	man, family, dream
o	odd, hot, watch		n	not, final, pan, knife
ō	old, oat, toe, low		ng	long, singer, pink
ô	coffee, all, taught, law, fought		p	pail, repair, soap, happy
ôr	order, fork, horse, story, pour		r	ride, parent, wear, more, marry
oi	oil, toy		s	sit, aside, pets, cent, pass
ou	out, now		sh	shoe, washer, fish, mission, nation
u	up, mud, love, double		t	tag, pretend, fat, button, dressed
ū	use, mule, cue, feud, few		th	thin, panther, both
ü	rule, true, food		th	this, mother, smooth
u̇	put, wood, should		v	very, favor, wave
ûr	burn, hurry, term, bird, word, courage		w	wet, weather, reward
ə	about, taken, pencil, lemon, circus		y	yes, onion
b	bat, above, job		z	zoo, lazy, jazz, rose, dogs, houses
ch	chin, such, match		zh	vision, treasure, seizure

DICTIONARY

A

ab•sorp•tion (ab sôrp´shən, ab zôrp´shən) *n.* The process of taking something in or soaking it up. page 119

ac•cel•er•ate (ak sel´ə rāt´) *v.* ac•cel•er•at•ed, ac•cel•er•at•ing To cause to go faster. page 114

ac•ces•si•ble (ak ses´ə bəl) *adj.* Easily obtained. page 114

ac•knowl•edge (ak nol´ij) *v.* ac•knowl•edged, ac•knowl•edg•ing To accept the reality or truth of. page 90

ad•e•quate•ly (ad´i kwət lē) *adv.* Sufficiently; well enough. page 47

ad•ja•cent (ə jā´sənt) *adj.* Next to; near. page 6

ad•mo•ni•tion (ad´mə nish´ən) *n.* Warning. page-109

a•dorn•ment (ə dôrn´mənt) *n.* Decoration. page-95

ad•ven•tur•er (ad ven´chər ər) *n.* A person who does unusual, exciting things. page 71

af•flic•tion (ə flik´shən) *n.* Illness. The boy's affliction made him unable to move. page 23

air•tight (âr´tīt´) *adj.* Not allowing air to get in or out. page 18

al•cove (al´kōv) *n.* A nook, or small roomlike place. page 66

a•lign•ment (ə līn´mənt) *n.* Arrangement in a straight line. The door would not close because it was out of alignment with the frame. page 78

al•ter•a•tion (ôl´tə rā´shən) *n.* Change. page 42

al•tim•e•ter (al tim´i tər, al´tə mē´tər) *n.* A device that measures altitude or height above the ground. page 114

ap•pli•ca•tion (ap´li kā´shən) *n.* The use to which something is put. page 47

art•ist•ry (är´tə strē) *n.* art•ist•ries Careful and skillful work in art. page 95

as•trol•o•gy (ə strol´ə jē) *n.* The study of the stars and planets by those who believe they influence human events. page 78

as•tro•nom•ic (as´trə nom´ik) *adj.* Having to do with stars and other heavenly bodies. page 12

at•tire (ə tīr´) *n.* Clothing. page 71

at•trib•ute (ə trib´ūt) *v.* at•trib•ut•ed, at•trib•ut•ing To name as a cause or source. In ancient times, people sometimes attributed earthquakes to angry gods. page 54

au•then•ti•cate (ô then´ti kāt´) *v.* au•then•ti•cat•ed, au•then•ti•cat•ing To prove; show to be true. page 54

au•to•mat•ed (ô´tə māt´ed) *adj.* Mechanical. page-30

B

bed•rock (bed´rok´) *n.* Solid rock just beneath the earth's surface. page 18

be•grudg•ing (bi gruj´ing) *adj.* Unwilling; reluctant. page 61

bi•zarre (bi zär´) *adj.* Very odd or strange. page 90

bra•va•do (brə vä´dō) *n.* The display of seeming bravery; boastfulness. page 60

C

cal•o•rie (kal´ə rē) *n.* A measure of food energy; the amount of energy used to raise the temperature of 1000 grams of water one degree Celsius. page 119

car•bo•hy•drate (kär´bō hī´drāt) *n.* A food sugar or starch found in candy, rice, bread, and other foods. page 119

cas•u•al•ty (kazh´ü əl tē) *n.* cas•u•al•ties Death or serious injury. page 18

cav•i•ty (kav´i tē) *n.* cav•i•ties A hole. page 61

cha•ris•ma (kə riz´mə) *n.* A strong and inspiring quality in a person that others like or follow. Manuel's charisma makes him the center of attention. page 12

cir•cum•stance (sûr´kəm stans´) *n.* The conditions surrounding an event. page 90

cit•a•del (sit´ə del) *n.* A fortress. page 95

clin•i•cal (klin´i kəl) *adj.* Having to do with the treatment of patients. Doctors tested the new drug in a clinical setting. page 23

co•in•ci•den•tal (kō in´si den´təl) *adj.* Happening at the same time but only by chance. page 90

col•o•nize (kol´ə nīz´) *v.* col•o•nized, col•o•niz•ing To settle a new country; establish a colony or community of people. page 95

com•mem•o•rate (kə mem´ə rāt´) *v.* com•mem•o•rat•ed, com•mem•o•rat•ing To honor the memory of. page 95

com•mod•i•ty (kə mod´i tē) *n.* com•mod•i•ties Something that can be bought and sold. Cars and TV sets are commodities that people can buy. page 102

com•pen•sate (kom´pən sāt´) *v.* com•pen•sat•ed, com•pen•sat•ing To make up for. page 102

com•pen•sa•tion (kom´pən sā´shən) *n.* Something offered as payment; something given to make up for a loss or injury. page 104

com•plex (kəm pleks´, kom´pleks) *adj.* Having many related parts; difficult to understand. page-104

com•plex•i•ty (kəm plek´si tē) *n.* com•plex•i•ties The state of being made up of many related parts. page 102

com•po•nent (kəm pō´nənt) *n.* Part. page 42

com•pound (kom´pound) *n.* Something made by combining two or more substances. page 108

com•prise (kəm prīz´) *v.* comprises Consists of; includes. page 18

con•cep•tu•al•ize (kən sep´chü ə līz´) *v.* con•cep•tu•al•ized, con•cep•tu•al•iz•ing To form an idea of. page 56

con•duct (kən dukt´) *v.* To lead or direct the course of. page 114

con•ser•va•tion•ist (kon´sər vā´shə nist) *n.* A person who works to preserve the environment. page 102

con•so•la•tion (kon sə lā´shən) *n.* Comfort. page 23

con•struc•tive (kən struk´tiv) *adj.* Causing improvement. page 47

con•sume (kən süm´) *v.* con•sumed, con•sum•ing To eat; use up. page 119

con•tem•po•rar•y (kən tem´pə rer´ē) *adj.* Belonging to today; of the present time. page 30

con•ven•ience (kən vēn´yəns) *n.* Freedom from effort or difficulty. page 30

con•ver•sion (kən vûr´zhən) *n.* The act of changing from one form or state to another. page 102

co•or•di•nat•ed (kō ôr´də nāt´id) *adj.* Working together in an orderly way. Moving the piano upstairs required the coordinated efforts of three people. page 12

coun•ter•clock•wise (koun´tər klok´wīz´) *adj.* Turning from right to left; in a direction opposite to the way the hands of a clock move. page 47

crim•i•nol•o•gy (krim´ə nol´ə jē) *n.* The scientific study of crime and criminals. page 42

cum•ber•some (kum´bər səm) *adj.* Awkward to carry. page 95

D

dank (dangk) *adj.* Unpleasantly cold and wet. page 71

de•fi•cien•cy (di fish´ən sē) *n.* de•fi•cien•cies A shortage; lack. page 119

dem•on•strate (dem´ən strāt´) *v.* dem•on•strat•ed, dem•on•strat•ing To show; prove. page 6

de•mon•stra•tive (di mon´strə tiv) *adj.* Openly showing one's feelings. page 8

den•si•ty (den´si tē) *n.* den•si•ties Thickness; the amount of something in a given space. page 18

de•scend (di send´) *v.* To go down. page 8

de•scen•dant (di sen´dənt) *n.* A person of a later generation of a family or group. page 6

de•spite (di spīt´) *prep.* In spite of. page 42

det•o•na•tor (det´ə nā´tər) *n.* A device that sets off explosives. page 109

di•ag•no•sis (dī´əg nō´sis) *n.* di•ag•no•ses A medical opinion concerning a person's health. The doctor's diagnosis was that she had the flu. page 23

di•ges•tion (di jes´chən, dī jes´chən) *n.* The process in the body that changes food to energy. page 119

di•lem•ma (di lem´ə) *n.* A difficult problem. page-42

dis•creet (di skrēt´) *adj.* Careful to behave appropriately. page 104

dis•cre•tion (di skresh´ən) *n.* The power to decide for oneself. page 102

E

ec•cen•tric (ek sen´trik) *adj.* Not traditional; out of the ordinary. page 109

ed•u•ca•tor (ej´ə kā´tər) *n.* A teacher. page 47

em•u•late (em´yə lāt´) *v.* em•u•lat•ed, em•ul•at•ing To imitate; try to be as good as. page 84

en•vi•sion (en vizh´ən) *v.* To form a picture of; imagine. page 42

en•zyme (en´zīm) *n.* A chemical in the body that breaks down food. page 119

e•qual•ize (ē´kwə līz´) *v.* e•qual•ized, e•qual•iz•ing To become the same or equal. page 61

es•tranged (e strānjd´) *adj.* No longer sharing affection; indifferent. The estranged brothers never saw or wrote to each other. page 85

e•volve (i volv´) *v.* e•volved, e•volv•ing To change slowly over time; work out gradually. page 109

ex•as•per•at•ed (eg zas´pə rāt´id) *adj.* Annoyed; irritated. page 36

ex•ca•va•tion (eks´kə vā´shən) *n.* Digging. page 18

ex•per•i•men•tal (ek sper´ə men´təl) *adj.* Used for testing; done in order to try something out. page 47

ex•plor•a•to•ry (ek splôr´ə tôr´ē) *adj.* Done in order to investigate or discover. page 60

F

fea•ture (fē´chər) *n.* An important or memorable part. page 66

fic•tion•al (fik´shə nəl) *adj.* Made-up; imaginary. page 84

fin•an•cier (fin´an sîr´, fī´nan sîr´) *n.* A person who takes part in financial matters involving large sums of money. page 108

fluke (flük) *n.* An odd event that is unlikely to happen again. page 37

fore•bear (fôr´bâr´) *n.* Ancestor; a person in the line of parents that led to the present generation. page 6

G

ge•o•ther•mal (jē´ō thûr´məl) *adj.* Having to do with the heat inside the earth. page 102

glitch (glich) *n.* An unexpected happening that causes a computer breakdown. page 37

H

har•ness (här´nis) *v.* To control in order to make use of. Sailboats harness the wind to move through the water. page 114

his•tor•ic (hi stôr´ik) *adj.* Very important; likely to be remembered for a long time. page 56

hos•pi•tal•ized (hos´pi tə līzd´) *adj.* In the hospital to receive treatment. page 23

I

i•den•ti•fi•ca•tion (ī den´tə fi kā´shən) *n.* The act of finding out who someone is. page 42

im•mersed (i mûrsd´) *adj.* Completely covered by a liquid. page 18

im•per•vi•ous (im pûr´vē əs) *adj.* Incapable of being passed through or penetrated. page 18

im•ply (im plī´) *v.* im•plied, im•ply•ing To suggest without being specific. page 78

in•com•pre•hen•si•ble (in´kom pri hen´sə bəl) *adj.* Not able to be understood. page 95

in•del•i•bly (in del´ə blē) *adv.* Permanently; in a way that cannot be erased or removed. Atomic energy has indelibly changed the course of history. page 54

in•de•scrib•a•ble (in´di skrī´bə bəl) *adj.* Not able to be described or put into words. page 71

in•fin•i•ty (in fin´i tē) *n.* in•fin•i•ties Endless number. page 13

i•ni•tia•tive (i nish´ə tiv) *n.* The willingness to take the first step toward doing something. page 47

in•scribe (in skrīb´) *v.* in•scribed, in•scrib•ing To carve letters or symbols in a hard surface. page-54

in•tact (in takt´) *adj.* Whole; not broken. page 78

in•te•grate (in´ti grāt´) *v.* in•te•grat•ed, in•te•grat•ing To bring different parts together to make a whole. page 30

in•ter•me•di•ar•y (in´tər mē´dē er´ē) *n.* in•ter•me•di•ar•ies Something or someone serving as a go-between. page 109

in•ti•mate (in´tə mit) *adj.* Familiar; personal. page-84

ir•i•des•cent (ir´i des´ənt) *adj.* Having many colors that change and shift; shimmering. The soap bubbles shone with iridescent colors. page 66

J

jour•nal•ist (jûr´nə list) *n.* Writer or reporter for a newspaper or magazine. page 84

K

key (kē) *v.* To type on a computer keyboard. page-37

ki•net•ic (ki net´ik) *adj.* Having to do with motion. page 114

L

la•bo•ri•ous (lə bôr´ē əs) *adj.* Requiring long, hard work. page 18

land•scape (land´skāp´) *n.* Scenery. page 66

lat•i•tude (lat´i tüd´, lat´i tūd´) *n.* An imaginary circle drawn around the earth at a given distance from the North or South Pole. page 6

light•weight (līt´wāt´) *adj.* Weighing very little. page 114

M

mag•nif•i•cence (mag nif´ə səns) *n.* Great beauty. page 66

mal•nu•tri•tion (mal´nü trish´ən, mal´nū trish´ən) *n.* Body condition that results when the foods necessary for good health are not eaten. page 119

map (map) *v.* mapped, map•ping To make a drawing, or map, of a place. page 71

maw (mô) *n.* The jaws and open mouth of an animal; an opening that looks like a large open mouth. page 61

mech•a•nized (mek´ə nīzd´) *adj.* Machine-run. page 114

me•tic•u•lous (mə tik´yə ləs) *adj.* Very careful about details; tidy. Jan was meticulous in picking up the tacks she had dropped. page 85

mi•grant (mī´grənt) *n.* A person who moves from one place to another, often in order to settle there; wanderer. page 6

mi•gra•tion (mī grā´shən) *n.* Movement from one place to settle in another place. page 8

min•us•cule (min´ə skūl´, mi nus´kūl) *adj.* Tiny; extremely small. page 12

mis•be•have (mis´bi hāv´) *v.* mis•be•haved, mis•be•hav•ing To act in a way that is not appropriate. page 37

mo•dem (mō´ dəm) *n.* A telephone device for sending data from one computer to another. page 30

mod•i•fy (mod´ə fī´) *v.* mod•i•fied, mod•i•fy•ing To change. page 114

mon•o•plane (mon´ə plān´) *n.* An aircraft that has only one set of wings. page 114

mon•u•men•tal (mon´yə men´təl) *adj.* Very large; huge. page 95

mo•ti•va•tion (mō´tə vā´shən) *n.* That which makes a person act; desire or drive. The wish to be first was his motivation for climbing the mountain. page 71

mul•ti•far•i•ous (mul´tə fâr´ē əs) *adj.* Many and varied. page 13

mys•ti•cal (mis´ti kəl) *adj.* Supernatural; spiritual. page 90

N

neu•rol•o•gy (nủ rol´ə jē, nyủ rol´ə jē) *n.* The branch of medicine that deals with the nervous system and its diseases. page 23

ni•tro•glyc•er•in (nī´trə glis´ər in) *n.* An explosive substance used in dynamite. page 108

no•mad (nō´mad) *n.* A member of a group that does not have a fixed home; a wanderer. page 8

no•mad•ic (nō mad´ik) *adj.* Wandering; having no fixed home. page 6

nu•tri•ent (nü´trē ənt, nū´trē ənt) *n.* Something that nourishes the body. page 119

O

o•cean•o•graph•ic (ō´shə nə graf´ik) *adj.* Having to do with the study and exploration of the world's oceans. page 90

op•ti•mis•tic (op´tə mis´tik) *adj.* Hopeful that things will turn out in the best possible way. page 23

out•mod•ed (out´mō´did) *adj.* Out-of-date; no longer used. page 30

P

par•a•ly•tic (par´ə lit´ik) *adj.* Unable to move. page 23

par•ish (par´ish) *n.* A district. page 84

pas•sage•way (pas´ij wā´) *n.* A way to get from one place to another. page 71

pass•word (pas´wûrd´) *n.* A code name; a secret word that authorizes a person to use a computer. page 36

pe•di•a•tri•cian (pē´dē ə trish´ən) *n.* A children's doctor. page 23

per•cep•tion (pər sep´shən) *n.* What is seen, heard, or detected by the body's senses. page 90

per•fo•rat•ed (pûr fə rā´tid) *adj.* Pierced; having holes. page 13

per•plexed (pər pleksd´) *adj.* Puzzled; confused. page 90

per•spec•tive (pər spek´tiv) *n.* Point of view. page-54

phe•nom•e•non (fə nom´ə non´) *n.* phe•nom•e•na, phe•nom•e•nons An event, especially one that is difficult to explain. page 90

plau•si•ble (plô´zə bəl) *adj.* Believable; easily accepted. The detective had a plausible explanation of how the crime was committed. page 85

po•rous (pôr´əs) *adj.* Full of very small holes. page 108

por•tray (pôr trā´) *v.* To describe using words, pictures, or actions. page 56

por•tray•al (pôr trā´əl) *n.* A description of something in the form of language or a picture. page 54

pre•cau•tion (pri kô´shən) *n.* Something done beforehand to prevent trouble. page 71

pre•con•cep•tion (prē´kən sep´shən) *n.* An idea of something formed before one has all the facts. page 54

pre•his•tor•ic (prē´his tôr´ik, prē´his tor´ik) *adj.* Happening before the time of recorded history; earlier than about 5000 B.C. page 54

pri•ma•ri•ly (prī mer´ə lē) *adv.* Mainly; for the most part. page 42

prob•a•ble (prob´ə bəl) *adj.* Likely; believable. page 6

pro•duc•tive (prə duk´tiv) *adj.* Having positive results; effective. page 18

pro•gram (prō´gram, prō´grəm) *n.* A set of instructions for a computer. page 36

pro•jec•tion (prə jek´shən) *n.* Prediction or plan for the future. Our projection is that Andy will win the election by 60 votes. page 42

pros•pec•tor (pros´pek tər, prə spek´tər) *n.* A person who searches for gold or other valuable things buried in the earth. page 71

pro•tein (prō´tēn) *n.* A nutrient that contains nitrogen and is found in meat, milk, eggs, and other foods. page 119

R

ra•di•ate (rā´dē āt´) *v.* ra•di•at•ed, ra•di•at•ing To branch out in different directions from a center area. page 66

ra•di•o•car•bon (rā´dē ō kär´bən) *n.* A substance that can be measured to find out the ages of ancient objects. page 78

ram•i•fi•ca•tion (ram´ə fi kā´shən) *n.* One of many possible different results. page 85

ref•u•gee (ref´yů jē´, ref´yů jē´) *n.* A person who flees his or her homeland and settles in another country. page 84

re•place•ment (ri plās´mənt) *n.* That which takes the place of something or someone else. page 30

re•plen•ish (ri plen´ish) *v.* To restore; add a new supply of. page 102

rev•e•la•tion (rev´ə lā´shən) *n.* New information. page 78

rev•o•lu•tion•ize (rev´ə lü´shə nīz´) *v.* rev•o•lu•tion•ized, rev•o•lu•tion•iz•ing To change greatly. page 30

rite (rīt) *n.* Ceremony. page 78

S

scru•ti•nize (skrü´tə nīz´) *v.* scru•ti•nized, scru•ti•niz•ing To examine closely; look at in detail. page 56

scru•ti•ny (skrü´tə nē) *n.* scru•ti•nies Close examination; study. page 54

sight•se•er (sīt´sē´ər) *n.* A person who visits a place of interest. page 78

sim•pli•fy (sim´plə fī´) *v.* sim•pli•fied, sim•pli•fy•ing To make easier or more simple. page 30

sit•u•ate (sich´ü āt´) *v.* sit•u•at•ed, sit•u•at•ing To locate. page 95

skep•ti•cal (skep´ti kəl) *adj.* Full of doubt; suspicious. page 37

snag (snag) *n.* A sharp or rough part of something that can catch and damage things. page 61

sol•stice (sol´stis, sōl´stis) *n.* The two times each year that the direct rays of the sun are farthest from the equator: June 21, the longest day of the year, and December 22, the shortest day of the year. page-78

spec•u•late (spek´yə lāt´) v. spec•u•lat•ed, spec•u•lat•ing To think or guess about something. Jerry speculates that one day people will live in space. page 90

spe•le•ol•o•gist (spē´lē ol´ə jist) n. A person who studies caves. page 60

spe•le•ol•o•gy (spē´lē ol´ə jē) n. The study of caves. page 66

spe•lunk•ing (spi lung´king) n. The exploration of caves. page 71

split sec•ond (split sek´ənd) n. A very small amount of time. page 47

sta•lac•tite (stə lak´tīt) n. A long, thin rock formation that extends down from a cave ceiling. page 66

sta•lag•mite (stə lag´mīt) n. A long, thin rock formation that extends up from the floor of a cave. page 66

stat•is•ti•cal (stə tis´ti kəl) adj. Having to do with numbers that measure and compare things. page-104

sta•tis•tics (stə tis´tiks) n. Numbers that measure and compare things. The team's statistics showed that Mel was the best player. page 102

strait (strāt) n. A narrow waterway that connects two larger bodies of water. page 6

stu•pen•dous (stü pen´dəs, stū pen´dəs) adj. Tremendous; astounding. page 37

sur•gi•cal (sûr´ji kəl) adj. Having to do with medical operations. page 23

sym•bol•ic (sim bol´ik) adj. Standing for something else. A flag is often symbolic of patriotism. page 95

sym•me•try (sim´i trē) n. An arrangement of parts in a mirrorlike way around a central point or line. page 78

T

trans•for•ma•tion (trans´fər mā´shən) n. A complete change. page 42

trans•form•er (trans fôr´mər) n. A device that changes electricity to make it suitable for home use. page 37

tran•sis•tor (tran zis´tər) n. A tiny device that controls the flow of electricity. page 47

trus•tee (trus tē´) n. A person who manages another's property. page 12

U

un•in•hab•it•a•ble (un´in hab´i tə bəl) adj. Not able to be lived in or on. page 8

un•in•hab•it•ed (un´in hab´i tid) adj. Without people; empty. page 6

un•leash (un lēsh´) v. To let loose; release. The speaker unleashed a torrent of angry words against his enemies. page 109

un•spoiled (un spoild´) adj. Not changed by humans in any way. page 66

u•til•i•ty (ū til´i tē) n. u•til•i•ties The state of being useful. page 30

V

var•i•a•ble (vâr´ē ə bəl) n. Something that changes, such as a number. The number of cars in the school parking lot is a variable. page 47

vi•al (vī´əl) n. A small bottle. page 13

vis•ta (vis´tə) n. View. page 12

vis•u•al•ize (vizh´ü ə līz´) v. vis•u•al•ized, vis•u•al•iz•ing To picture in one's mind. page 54

W

waste•ful (wāst´fəl) adj. Using more than necessary; marked by waste. page 102

welt (welt) n. A raised place on the skin caused by an injury. page 60

whet (hwet, wet) v. whet•ted, whet•ting To sharpen; make eager. Eating one hamburger whetted his appetite for another one. page 60